TOP TIPS FOR NEW TEACHERS

ED WATSON

SILVERDALE PUBLICATIONS

A CIP catalogue record for this title is available from the British Library.

First published in Great Britain in 2020 by Silverdale Publications.

ISBN 978-1-8380949-0-4

ISBN (ebook) 978-1-8380949-1-1

CONTENTS

INTRODUCTION

The very fact you have decided to read this book tells me you are going to be an amazing teacher. How do I know that? The best teachers are the ones who are willing to learn, to try new techniques and learn on the job, and they are humble enough to know they are not the finished article. By reading this book, you are taking the first step.

Everyone who walks on this planet makes mistakes. Every teacher who has ever taught in a classroom makes mistakes. I cannot promise that you will be immune from making your own, but by considering my advice, you will have a better idea of the common mistakes teachers do make and you will know how to train yourself to avoid them.

You can read this book from start to finish or in discrete chunks. Whichever way you choose, I hope you can learn from my experiences to maximise the chances of you finding your feet as quickly as possible in the classroom.

The book is divided into nine chapters with concepts taken from my experiences within the classroom and from visiting high-performing schools across the country. I love to learn; I have read hundreds of teaching and learning books and have condensed my knowledge into this handbook for all teachers entering the profession.

I must stress that this book and its advice is suitable for all teachers, whether teaching primary or secondary pupils. Where advice seemingly references secondary school environments, my hope is that primary teachers will be able to take the advice on board and apply it to their own settings.

Chapter 1 looks into how to cultivate your ideal classroom environment. It explores the power of observing other teachers and being observed yourself, building effective relationships with pupils, and how to approach improving your own practice to maximise your progress.

Chapter 2 focuses on behaviour management techniques to ensure your class is under total control. The chapter contains many Top Tips to ensure you maintain excellent behaviour management in your classroom whilst retaining your own personality and teaching style.

Chapter 3 highlights the importance of routines to support the high behavioural expectations you will set within your classroom. Different routines are suggested and explored to improve your practice, alongside advice about creating and instilling your own routines within your own context.

Chapter 4 explores ideas of pedagogy and common pitfalls that new and trainee teachers make when they first enter the classroom. Eager to please pupils, colleagues and their university tutors, trainee teachers often try to do too much when in reality, less is more. This chapter explores the main ideas of effective pedagogy and balances this with the understanding that learning to teach takes a significant amount of time, while acknowledging that progress can be accelerated by taking the advice in this book on board.

Chapter 5 offers general advice that any teacher should

know but which many teacher training routes don't explore in great detail. It emphasises the importance of working effectively with colleagues and explores how you can look after your own career development.

Chapter 6 considers the career advice that is often overlooked during training. It walks you through the teaching application process, the interview process and how to leave a job in the best possible manner. It finishes with advice on taking the next steps in your career, whether that is within teaching or into leadership.

Chapter 7 concerns pay and the common myths that surround it. Used correctly, this chapter may give you thousands of pounds of additional income over a year, and tens of thousands over the course of your career. The ideas within this chapter are rarely talked about, are not known by many teachers and are not, understandably, regularly publicised by headteachers. For some, the techniques in this chapter will reap major rewards.

Chapter 8 explores ways to maximise your personal productivity. Teaching is a demanding job, but you must use your time wisely. Without restraint, you may end up spending too much of your time on schoolwork and not enough time looking after yourself. This chapter gives you some tried and tested ideas to maximise productivity whilst still achieving a significant impact in your role.

Chapter 9 further develops the theme of personal productivity by looking at ways to protect your personal wellbeing. As a teacher, it is vital that you put yourself first. Without an effective teacher in front of them, pupils will not learn much. It is far better to be a fresh teacher with an average lesson, than a tired teacher with an amazing lesson.

The book concludes by summarising the ideas that have been discussed. It would be fantastic to hear your thoughts and comments on the book, so please do message me through my social media channels.

Throughout the book, there will be regular opportunities to tweet me; if you can include the hashtag #TeachingTopTip, it will ensure I can access the comments more easily. If you could also leave a review on the site where you bought this book, that would be greatly appreciated. The feedback is useful for developing future editions of the book, and it helps share advice to a wider audience.

BECOMING AN EXCELLENT TEACHER

H ave you ever had a nightmare where you are in front of a class of pupils who are totally out of control, and you are powerless to do anything? Don't fret. A lot of new teachers experience this. Surprisingly, it is also common to hear this story in the staff room at the start of every academic year when teachers return after a six-week break. It turns out even experienced teachers can be nervous about having new classes and setting new standards, even if they have been teaching for years.

Nervousness is not something to fear; it is perfectly normal and can help focus the senses. One of the greatest tips for effective classroom management is to have a clear mental picture of how you want your class to look in the future. Knowing precisely what routines your pupils should follow and exactly what should happen at each stage of the lesson will lead to a degree of automation in your teaching that will allow you to operate at a high level.

This is a tactic that experienced teachers fall back on year after year. They have built up this visualisation, having already practised it on previous classes. They start each year knowing that even if their classes are not where they want them to be, they will be there in a short while.

But, I hear you ask, how do you know what you want if you are new to the classroom? It's all down to the power of observations.

OBSERVATIONS

OBSERVE OTHERS

As a fresh-faced young teacher entering the profession, I had a vague idea of what I wanted my classroom to look like and how I wanted pupils to behave in class. But this all drained away as soon as my first pupils entered the classroom.

Indeed, many of the mistakes newer teachers make are simply the result of inexperience; they will improve with time. But how do we accelerate this progression to make our lives easier, sooner?

During your training years, your timetable is likely to be as light as it is ever going to be. Although you may seem extremely busy, dropping in to as many teachers' lessons as possible over the course of the year will allow you to poach good practice from the best teachers and identify learning points from the weakest. Use it as a development opportunity to enhance your own practice and to test these tactics with your own classes.

Observations of other teachers don't need to be for the whole lesson. Try dropping in for ten minutes and noting down anything of interest. Then follow this up with the teacher afterwards if you have any questions. I've found that most teachers are fine with you visiting for five or ten minutes but be sure to give them advance notice. Some teachers are more than happy for you to just drop in unannounced but for others this may raise their anxiety levels, so it is always worthwhile to catch them beforehand to check they are comfortable with it.

One of my top tips is to observe as many teachers as you possibly can, whether or not they teach 'your subject'. Trust me, there are some incredible teachers in every school and you can glean so much from them. The lessons may appear to be run so smoothly, with everything under control, that trying to understand how it got to this stage may be difficult to the untrained eye. You must therefore question them at every opportunity, for example: Why did you stand there when you say that? Was there a reason for ignoring him when he did this? Why are you questioning those pupils in that way? Be curious. Probe. Ask questions and you will be rewarded.

On the flipside, there are unfortunately some weaker teachers out there as well.

Before I continue, I must say that the chances are very high that you will be terrible when you first start teaching. There, I've said it. What you need to know, though, is that most of us were poor to start with and the advice in this book will help you accelerate your own progress. I certainly look back at my first few months in teaching and know that I made a lot of mistakes. But I don't think we should look back with embarrassment; these mistakes make you a better teacher and learning from them is how you develop your professional teaching.

Now as I've said, there are some weak teachers in schools up and down the country. It doesn't matter whether you teach in a public, state or any school for that matter, we have all experienced some poorer teachers from our own school days, so it's not surprising they still exist as colleagues.

However, hold your fire. You can often learn the most from poor teachers. Observing those who struggle to explain concepts, identify misbehaviour and achieve simple class management can often provide more clues on how to teach than watching someone who appears to have everything under control. You can spot flaws more easily in weaker teachers and avoid them in your own practice.

Why are they throwing paper aeroplanes around? Why are they not doing the work? Was the explanation clear enough? Were they paying attention when the teacher was speaking? Did the teacher get everyone silent before speaking? Are pupils talking over the teacher? These are just a selection of questions you can ask yourself when observing teachers who are struggling to control their classes.

In contrast, there are some excellent teachers from whom you can learn a huge amount. In my experience, I've found that the teachers who appear to be in control the most, who achieve the best results for their pupils and whose relationships with pupils are excellent, have a reason for everything they do. I remember asking a teacher why he always seemed to have the windows open in his classroom. His answer astounded me. He said, 'If they're not going to listen to me talking, I would rather they were distracted by the cold than anything else!'

Now, many of you will disagree with this, and I am not convinced it is the right attitude myself. But the fact that he had thought about his classroom in this level of detail is the reason he is one of the best teachers I have ever come across. His teaching was exceptional because he had made a series of small decisions that culminated in a highly effective classroom operation that worked for him.

Top Tip: Observe teachers across all disciplines. If you're a maths teacher, look at what teachers in Humanities, English, Arts and Science do. The best teachers can poach ideas from everyone and use them in their own practice. #TeachingTopTip

Be observed

All criticism is constructive. At least that's how I see it. If you take criticism constructively, you will accelerate your progress. When you first start teaching, you will make mistakes. Colleagues around you have years of experience and their opinions are valid. Some suggestions may be easier to take than others, but if you make an effort to listen to all of them, you will improve dramatically. Be humble. It takes a rare teacher to walk into a school and nail it from day one without any help from anyone. In fact, I don't think it's possible. Use the wisdom gained from colleagues over time to your advantage. You won't get far trying to do it all yourself.

Humility can go a long way. There is nothing more soul destroying and frustrating for a school leader than giving up their own time to develop teachers when the person they are trying to help has the blinkers up; it feels like they are talking to a brick wall. As a school leader and leader of a department, one of the best parts of my job is developing the practices of other teachers and coaching them to find gains that will improve their teaching. However, it is very frustrating when teachers refuse to take advice on board and think they are the finished product already.

Remember, criticism is professional, not personal. When you receive tough criticism, it is usually a sign that the person giving it cares and wants to help you improve. Some people don't see that. Don't be one of them; take the advice on the chin. Trust their experience, especially at the start when you're learning the craft. They can see things and behaviours that you can't just yet. Be humble. It will pay dividends in the long run.

SET THE STANDARD

In a classroom environment, culture always wins. One of the best pieces of advice I received early in my career was from one of my old teachers.

He said, 'Ed, remember, in every classroom there are two individuals that will keep on working even if a bomb goes off in the classroom. There are another two intent on misbehaving, who don't want to be there. And then there are the rest.'

As my experience has grown, this has resonated. As teachers, we must try and get 'the rest' on side. By doing so, we create cultural norms in our classroom which will lead to the mischievous two having to toe the line. If as a teacher you can create the 'it's just how we do it around here,' then those two will have to follow your class approach and the culture is set.

Alternatively, if you don't keep the two misbehaving pupils under control, the rest of the class are likely to side with them. Instead of having two pupils misbehaving, you quickly end up with five, six or seven. When teachers complain that their class is feral, or completely out of control, it is usually because the teacher hasn't got a handle on the two who started it. Get those under control, and the rest will be on your side.

The second thing to remember is what I term the 'heliotropic effect.' Plants move towards the light, wherever the light may be. From experience, pupils radiate towards positivity. Rather than issuing instructions such as 'don't do this' or 'don't do that', it can be much more powerful to enforce the desired behaviours you want by praising the pupils who are doing what you request. Nine times out of ten when you are admonishing a class, the vast majority will be doing what you want. Praising the specific individuals who are doing what you have asked them to can lead to other pupils copying them, as they would also like to be singled out for praise.

DEVELOP EFFECTIVE RELATIONSHIPS

Effective relationships between pupils and teachers are at the heart of teaching. As a teacher, your aim should be to gain your pupils' respect, not to be their friend. This doesn't mean you're not interested in them; it's quite the opposite. I've always found a very small investment in pupils can reap massive dividends for classroom management later down the line. Yet it is important this boundary stays firm, otherwise it can be harder for teachers to discipline pupils when required.

As I've said, there will be two or three pupils in every class who are likely to be the troublemakers. These are the pupils you want to get on your side straight away. They don't require any special treatment in the classroom and should be sanctioned in the same way as other pupils. However, if you can get them on side early on, they will make your life so much easier by bringing the remaining pupils with them.

So, I can hear you ask, how do we get these troublemakers on side? Well, a helpful start would be to ask them what hobbies they have, whether they like sport, what they're doing on the weekend, or similar questions. Engaging with them outside of your subject or simply as their teacher is a good way to learn a bit more about them. Once you've engaged them in a conversation about their interests, the key is then to listen and make a written or mental, note of what they have said. Then, after the weekend or a week later, the key is to ask how their hobby is going or how their match went.

This may sound manipulative, but it's merely engaging with the pupils on another level. They will respect you much more; no longer are you just Mr Watson who teaches them maths every day. Instead, you are Mr Watson who asks them how their football is going, whether they are riding their bike with friends on the weekend, who knows it's their birthday next Friday, as well as someone who also happens to teach them.

In my first year, I had an extremely challenging class to manage, and they seemed to be getting the better of me every lesson. I was always nervous before teaching them. But after speaking to the pupils in the class, I realised they were the stars of their rugby team. So, I invested time in watching their rugby matches after school and attended their county final. All of this helped build relationships with these pupils and it helped win their respect. This took time, but it was worth it. The effort spent at the beginning of a year building relationships and getting to know pupils helps you in the long run, and the pupils will often give you so much more in return.

I must stress that asking them about their hobby or their weekend once won't make a lot of difference; they will see right through you. Some pupils have so many different people coming in and out of their lives that they won't fully trust or respect you until they know you are sticking around. This may take up to a year if I'm honest, in the knowledge that you'll be around the following academic year, but it can be fast-tracked if you make the effort.

When I've spoken to teachers and colleagues who are finding behaviour management difficult, I stress the importance of building relationships with pupils and taking an interest in them as individuals. Some have responded with, 'but that takes effort.' Therein lies the problem. Put simply, a small effort to get know and relate to pupils will make your job much easier and save time. Unfortunately, some teachers just can't seem to see the long-term benefit.

Top Tip: Call pupils' homes in the first week. This is an invaluable tip for a new teacher. You won't be ringing just any pupil, only those who immediately appear difficult. Are these hard to spot? No, not at all. You will soon gain a sense of the pupils who are likely to cause you trouble in lessons. Try to ring their home on one of the very first days you teach them.

Counter-intuitively, these phone calls should be very positive about the pupil, explaining what a pleasure it is to teach them and what amazing enthusiasm they showed in today's lesson. Often the parents of these pupils have received frequent negative phone calls from disgruntled teachers, so to hear a positive phone call can build a good relationship. I remember calling a Year 10 girl's father once and the father nearly broke down in tears saying that it had been the first time any teacher in the school had said anything positive about his daughter.

You know this pupil may cause some trouble down the line, but you have built up a positive relationship with their parents first, which means they are far more likely to support you in managing their child's challenging behaviour. It really does work. Finally, if you are making a positive phone call, make sure it is only positive. Leave any criticism for another day. #TeachingTopTip

---

'DON'T SMILE 'TIL CHRISTMAS'

There is a popular adage amongst the teaching profession that in your first term as a teacher, trainee or even at a new school, you should be very strict until Christmas. There are two ways to look at this.

Firstly, even when you are trying to set boundaries in the early stages of teaching a class, never forget to use your sense of humour if a situation requires it. Don't be a wooden plank. If something is funny, laugh, otherwise pupils will find you weird. Having a sense of humour can open you up to certain pupils and make you more personable and relatable, which can help your classroom management.

Taken literally, the idea of keeping up a stern façade until Christmas sounds as if it can do more harm than good. But if you read it as meaning that you should start by setting strict boundaries and not relaxing them for a significant period, it absolutely makes sense. Teachers are not the pupils' friends. Pupils don't want you to be a friend; they want you to be warm and fair, and they want to learn. If you can achieve these three wishes, they will respect you, which in my view is ultimately what every teacher should aim for. But achieving those three aims is easier said than done.

It is human nature for pupils to test any teacher in front of them, to see what they can and can't get away with. Growing up ourselves, we have all been pupils with certain teachers and have seen how far we can push it. As a teacher, however, no matter how good you are (or were in a previous school), when you arrive with a new class you have no reputation and must start from scratch. Therefore, you need to be strict and you must set clear boundaries.

Loosening up and relaxing too soon as a teacher, avoiding sanctions too soon because you think the pupils 'like you' is a recipe for disaster and gives you little room to manoeuvre in the future. By starting strictly, you can lighten up later, which is more straightforward. However, if you start with no boundaries, introducing them later can be a painful process.

Remember, you are not their friend, you are in charge of their learning. Yes, be personable, relatable and have a laugh, but also bear in mind you are seeking their respect.

Top Tip: Set strict boundaries early on and stick to them for a significant period. When you take over a new class, you need to set the ground rules to ensure your pupils follow your high expectations. You should ensure you are consistent with these rules and resist the temptation to relax them too quickly. It is much easier to relax rules than to implement them, so never be tempted to give too much back too soon. #TeachingTopTip

---

SENSE OF HUMOUR

Now, it is pointless me telling you to use a sense of humour with pupils if you don't have one. If you try and manufacture one it will not work, and you may look silly. However, if you do have a natural sense of humour, try and use it when speaking to pupils to help build positive relationships. Around school, when dealing with incidents, the respect you have earned through building effective relationships with pupils can help you manage the situation. Your school may have black and white lines which don't give you much wriggle room in how you manage the behaviour, but there is always a personable way to offer sanctions or praise and it definitely goes a long way with pupils. Be yourself, but remember you are their teacher, not their friend.

Sarcasm and its danger

Be careful when using your sense of humour. Some pupils can take sarcasm and wit literally and it can land teachers in trouble. I'm not saying don't use it; I'm advising caution.

It is about being careful with your language and knowing your pupils. Telling a pupil they look like they've been dragged through a bush because their top button isn't done up and their shirt is hanging out depends on you knowing the pupil well. Having said that, were a pupil or parent to write a complaint or e-mail you to clarify your comments, it doesn't look great on paper.

This is just something to be mindful of, not to worry about, but just be aware that verbal comments can be misinterpreted. Be careful.

Top Tip: Use your sense of humour wisely. If you have one, it can be used as a great strength in dealing and reacting to many scenarios. However, do be mindful of comments that you make, because when taken literally and out of context, they can look inappropriate. Also, make sure you don't use your sense of humour to shirk necessary sanctions. **#TeachingTopTip**

PRACTICE DOESN'T MAKE PERFECT, IT MAKES PERMANENT

Experience doesn't necessarily make you a better teacher. Yes, it gives you a different perspective and inevitably helps you improve you in certain areas, but as someone once told me, it is much better to be a teacher who learns every year for three years than one who teaches for 25 years and repeats their first year 25 times.

That has stuck with me. I think to be an extraordinary teacher, you need to be searching for continuous improvement in everything you do.

Teaching again and again, year after year, without changing anything is not going to make you a better teacher. You need to practise to improve and you need to reflect, observe and be observed to accelerate your progress.

You need to find the single, most important factor that will develop your teaching and work on that alone until you have improved it. It is how you improve at anything. Athletes or musicians don't improve by playing full matches or concerts all the time. Instead, they practise the small constituent parts first until they have mastered those, and then bring it all together. Do the same with your teaching.

I found I developed my teaching skills more rapidly by having meetings with a mentor, someone I trusted from my department. We would both sit down and identify the single most important target for that week. Then, once I was consciously aware of what I was working on, I could improve at a much faster rate. For me to make this progress, I needed to keep it in my consciousness. I used to have a laminated piece of card on my classroom door with my target written on it, to remind me of it every time I walked into my classroom.

Using this system, I absolutely loved developing myself as a teacher.

Once you have worked on one target, you can try something else each week and before you know it, you will have mastered lots of different skills and will be an accomplished practitioner in the classroom.

Top Tip: Improvement poster on the door. When you have identified the single biggest factor that will improve your teaching, write it on a piece of paper, laminate it and stick it on the outside of your classroom door so it is visible to everyone. If you are concerned that pupils may know you are working on something you don't want them to see, phrase the improvements in a coded way. This is a fantastic way of holding yourself accountable for what you're working on, keeping it in your conscious thought. It also helps leaders, mentors and colleagues to see what you are aiming for; when they drop in on your lessons, they can focus on observing this element in particular. #TeachingTopTip

---

LEARN FROM YOUR MISTAKES

We all try things in our classroom that just don't work. If you see everything you do as a learning opportunity, then you can remain positive in your teaching. Whatever your mistake is, if you learn from it and endeavour to never repeat it, you will prosper. And if you never make mistakes, then you're not trying hard enough to develop your practice.

One of my mistakes occurred during my first year of

teaching with my most difficult class, my Year 8 pupils. They were high attaining pupils so were sharp and skilled at concealing poor behaviour. The school I trained in had a behaviour system, but I struggled to use it to control the class at first, and I used to dread teaching them. I frequently had them after lunch and would sit in the classroom before they came in, dreading the bell that would herald their arrival.

My mistake was that during one lesson, I got so fed up because they weren't listening to me that for the first (and only) time ever, I lost my temper and shouted at the class to be quiet. I had lost control of them in that moment. As soon as I did it, one of the pupils looked at me and I could tell she was taken aback by it. In that split second, I knew I had made a mistake and would never repeat it.

The crucial thing was that as soon as the lesson had finished, I reflected on the incident for hours, days and weeks. Fine, I'd done something that I wasn't proud of and was regretting it, but I treated it like a learning experience. Why did it end like that? Could I have done something differently? Did I miss behaviour leading up to that?

One of the things I did to turn this situation around was to observe this class with another member of staff who had them under absolute control. I observed the class for a whole hour's lesson and was hurt. The pupils that were causing me so much grief were behaving impeccably for this teacher down the corridor and I felt like I was a rubbish teacher for a moment. But then I decided to think positively. If the other teacher could control them, then so could I. Observing this colleague helped me; now I knew the standard the pupils were capable of, I didn't need to take any more of their nonsense. Once the pupils knew this, their game was up. It took a few more weeks or months, but by the end of the year they were absolutely where they needed to be.

It also taught me another learning point. When you are training, your worst, most behaviourally taxing class will be the one you learn the most from when you look back on it. Of course, it's easy to say this with hindsight, but you will realise years later that they helped shape you the most in improving your practice.

'CHIN UP.' IT'S NEVER AS BAD AS IT SEEMS IN THE MOMENT.

The Car Crash lesson. Oh dear. We dread it. The lesson where everything goes wrong. Looking back, though, they turn out to be the most hilarious and are often a gift for any dinner party you attend. Retelling stories of your teaching failures can entertain many people for hours, yet at the time you may be standing there just willing time to speed up.

I vividly remember my first disastrous lesson. As soon as it ended, I went to the staff room to tell everyone about it and was distinctly underwhelmed by their response. I expected staff to console me, ask questions about it and be worried for me. And yet that wasn't how they reacted. It felt as if my story was normal, a rite of passage. Every teacher has had a lesson like this at some point and it turns out to be completely uneventful.

I don't want you to feel that colleagues will ignore you; of course you will have colleagues who will listen to a debrief and talk it through with you. It's just that all teachers have been there and done it. It is part of the learning experience, so it's nothing to worry about. Remember, treat everything like a learning experience. Reflect. What did I do wrong? Was I prepared enough? Was the work too easy or too difficult for them? Did I cope with misbehaviour well enough? What can I do differently to avoid a repeat performance?

I remember being told in my training that teaching has so

many ups and downs, but I didn't expect so many in a week, let alone in a day. They even exist within a lesson. Try not to take it too seriously when things aren't going so well. You may be going through a tricky patch with a particular class, but the advice in this book will enable you to reduce the length of this spell and ensure you get the class where you want them to be as quickly as possible.

I remember once teaching another tricky Year 8 class who were making shapes using a pair of compasses. As a maths teacher, you learn soon enough to avoid saying something like, 'Make sure you don't stab everyone with the compasses', because that is exactly what they will do. The lesson had gone for about 45 minutes without incident. Then someone called me over to see one of the pupils who was sitting on the front row near the board with his hand up and his other hand covering his eye. His friend next to him said, 'Tom has just stabbed himself in the eye with a compass.' My first reaction was not, are you ok?' but 'What on earth did you do that for?'

He replied, 'I wanted to know if it would hurt.'

In the end, it didn't amount to anything, and he was absolutely fine, but in that split second the lesson had changed course and my heart sank. Nevertheless, as I said earlier, it turned out to be an entertaining anecdote at many dinner parties to come.

At the start of your teaching journey, it feels like you are on an emotional rollercoaster where every day or every minute is either a euphoric high or a dismal low. What experience gives you is the flattening of these emotions. Highs and lows still happen, but they affect you less. This is how teachers achieve longevity in their careers. I'm definitely not saying it becomes any less enjoyable, but the emotional ups and downs don't take over as much when you know it is all part of a journey.

MANAGING BEHAVIOUR

BE 100% SURE

Before I delve into many of the best strategies I've found to manage behaviour, one of the essential elements of behaviour management is that when you are issuing sanctions, you must be absolutely certain that you have identified the right individual with your own eyes. If pupils suspect that you could not possibly have seen the incident, they will often wriggle out of sanctions. If you can't say for certain that it was definitely them, how can they be sanctioned for something that you think they did but are not 100% sure about?

Many of these strategies and techniques are therefore designed to allow you to see misbehaviour with your own eyes, so that you can dismiss any complaint or argument made by a pupil. It sounds simple, but it isn't!

There will be times where you are 99% sure someone has said or done something but you have not seen it. Can you punish them severely if you are not 100% sure it was them? I don't think you can. Try and see the behaviour with your own eyes and it will prevent many problems in the future.

Top Tip: Be 100% certain before issuing a sanction. It will save many problems down the line and prevents you from sanctioning the wrong pupil. #TeachingTopTip

---

STATE BEHAVIOUR AS A FACT

You should avoid getting into a debate with a pupil, whether you are a trainee, newly qualified or an experienced teacher. It can inflame situations and lead to an unnecessary debate that pleases nobody. Instead, clearly stating the facts of what somebody is doing and why it is or isn't what you would like in your classroom leaves little room for a pupil to negotiate.

'Billy, you're being rude,' is a sentence that Billy could argue with. He is likely to respond with, 'No, I'm not!' Here, the teacher has given an opinion and not a fact.

In the teacher's opinion, Billy is being rude, but Billy might not think this at all. From Billy's perspective, this could be how he speaks at home to his siblings or how his parents speak to him. Therefore, as a teacher, this comment could inflame the situation, as it allows Billy a retort.

Alternatively, stating 'Billy, you're talking whilst I'm talking. The expectation is that in this classroom only one person speaks at a time, therefore I have no choice but to issue your first warning,' offers no room for manoeuvre from Billy. The teacher has stated that Billy was talking, and if this was the case, Billy has no room for disagreement. Re-affirming the expected behaviour not only reminds Billy of his responsibilities for future behaviour but it also acts as a reminder to the rest of the pupils in the class. This is a much better way of managing behaviour and reduces the chances of a confrontation.

Here is another example. When you see a pupil throwing a paper aeroplane, instead of saying 'David, that was dangerous; this is your first warning,' you could say, 'David, you have thrown a paper aeroplane across the classroom. The expectation is that in this classroom no one throws anything. This is your first warning.'

This is a much better response, because it states the behaviour as a fact, reminds him and the class of the expectation and follows up with an unemotional sanction. While it may take slightly longer to say, it offers huge dividends and gives pupils little wriggle room to argue with decisions you have made. You can give sanctions and admonishments without emotion; you are merely stating facts and saying that a pupil hasn't met those expectations. There is nothing more to it.

When I was at secondary school, we had a pupil called Alex who was one of the sharpest pupils in the year and also very quick-witted. We had a physics teacher who struggled to control us and would frequently raise her voice to try and settle us. Once, she lost her temper and raged, 'Stop it! This is not a pantomime!'

Quick as a flash, Alex responded, 'Oh, yes it is!'

This light-hearted example, although not rude or malicious, offers a prime example of a teacher issuing a statement that a pupil can disagree with. Instead, state the misbehaviour as a fact, so that there is no wriggle room for a pupil to argue their case.

MEAN WHAT YOU SAY

CHECK FOR COMPLIANCE

After issuing instructions, it is vital to check that pupils are following them. One way of doing this is to issue an instruction which gives you a way to check it has been done. For example, if you want pupils to copy down a paragraph that you have written on the board, and then to look at you to await their next instruction, you could ask them to put their pens down. This makes it easy for you to see when pupils have finished the task without you having to say anything more.

It is not enough to merely ask them to work in silence; you need to watch for people who are talking. Spotting the first pupil who opens their mouth offers you a golden opportunity to sanction them and to reinforce your expectation. If everyone in the classroom has heard someone break the silence and you do not sanction it, it shows the pupils that you don't really mean what you say, and they won't take you seriously when you ask for silence in the future.

Failing to check for compliance after issuing an expectation seemingly gives pupils a choice to do as they're told or not, which is definitely not your intention.

Importantly, issuing instructions such as asking for silence should never become punitive actions; they should always be delivered positively. This perspective is often difficult to comprehend, but pupils hate having something done to them. There is a fine line between achieving productive work and pupils feeling oppressed.

For example, when asking for silence I explain that 'we' are in silence, not 'you' are in silence. I feel this helps promote a classroom culture of a joint effort where we all want everybody to succeed. Also, explaining that we are going to work in silence to re-focus or get some good work done also helps narrate the 'why', rather than saying the whole class are working in silence for ten minutes because they've been so poorly behaved. The latter will just breed resentment and you will spend ten minutes wrestling with the class to stop talking during silence.

Top Tip: Mean what you say. If you have issued an instruction, take some time to check that pupils are doing what you have asked them to. Pupils need to know that you are serious about it. If you ask for silence, but allow whispering, pupils are less likely to follow your next instruction. **#TeachingTopTip**

BE AUTHORITATIVE WITHOUT BEING AGGRESSIVE

Pupils will get away with as much as you allow; they will rise and fall to the expectations that you set for the class. If you let them do something, they will. If you don't, they won't.

In your classroom, you are the boss and that's the end of it. You make the rules, you administer the rules and that should be that. If you state your expectations clearly enough and follow them through consistently, you should be able to manage your classroom effectively. One of the key problems that teachers experience at the start of their careers is not being taken seriously. Commanding respect from the class through your voice is something that needs to be honed over time, but there are a few key pointers.

Stand still and only talk when there is absolute silence. *Never* speak over people. It can be excruciating waiting for the class to be silent, but it has to be done. If you allow someone to speak over you, even for a second, your authority will be diminished. Be courageous and bide your time. Then when you have started to speak, if anyone speaks over you, just stop and remind the class of your expectations.

Know what you are aiming for. What do you want the class to do and how do you expect them to do it? Do you need them to be silent or quiet? Or do paired work? The more explicit you can make your instructions, the better your classroom management will be.

Top Tip: Replace 'please' with 'thank you'. 'Please can you take your coat off?' is a plea for support from a pupil. It can lack conviction and is almost a request for a pupil to comply rather than an instruction. Replacing please with a thank you at the end assumes compliance and is often far more effective. Saying, 'Can you take your coat off, thank you,' leaves the pupil with less of an option to say no, and often leads to much greater compliance. 'Pens down now, thank you,' sounds more confident and assumes compliance from your pupils. #TeachingTopTip

---

OFFER CHOICES WHERE YOU'RE HAPPY WITH BOTH OUTCOMES

One useful way of managing some trickier scenarios in your class is to offer them a choice where you will be happy with both outcomes. Pupils like to feel they're in control and that they have a choice in the matter.

Telling a pupil they must sit in a certain seat next to an individual they don't particularly like, with no alternative, is often a recipe for disaster. Instead, offering a choice for that pupil to either sit in that seat or next to another pupil who you are equally happy for them to work beside is a completely different ball game. You have now offered that pupil a choice of two seats. Strange as it sounds, you will find that pupil much more likely to sit in one of the two seats without fuss.

This offer of choice where you're happy with both outcomes arises in so many parts of school life that it is an excellent tactic to add to your armoury. Offering pupils such a choice is a lot better than telling them where they should sit or what they should be doing.

However, this is not always possible. If a pupil needs to sit somewhere or do something and there is no alternative, that pupil has to follow your instructions, otherwise you will have to follow through with your school's behaviour policy. Giving a choice is merely a good technique for the occasions when you are genuinely not that bothered which option they take. It gives pupils the feeling that they are in control when realistically, you as the teacher still hold all the cards.

Some may ask what happens if a pupil is still not happy with the two choices you offered? Well, you should stand your ground. If you have offered two choices but they don't like either, then you should stay put and insist they choose one of the two options (the lesser of two evils for them perhaps). Pupils may kick up a bit of a fuss, but from experience, even though they won't know why, they do understand they have been given a choice and therefore they will usually take up the offer. Again, if they don't, follow the school behaviour policy; you can't be seen to give up too much control to pupils who somehow think they are in charge of the classroom or the situation.

. . .

THE SHORT RETORT

It's advisable to have some short, sharp phrases that can be used as replies to pupils when they challenge you. You might struggle to come up with any yourself, but through observations you can pick up some that are effective and try them yourself. They can be highly personal; phrases others use, or the suggestions I make below, may not feel right to you. That is absolutely fine; find some that work well for you.

'I've asked you to come here so I can speak to you, not for you to speak to me.'

'I've asked you, and now I'm telling you...'

'I'm not entering into a discussion; this is my decision and it is not going to change.'

These retorts may jar with some readers. That is fine. For me, they work well but I can understand that they may not fit everyone's personality or teaching style. That is to be expected. The point still stands that you should build a collection of short, sharp retorts or comments that work for you in diffusing difficult scenarios, in your context and with your personality.

GENERAL TIPS

PUPILS ARRIVING LATE

There is a pretty high chance that you will be confronted with pupils arriving late to your lesson at some point. As a new teacher with a new class, a late pupil offers a great chance to assert your authority and reprimand them for being late. However, it can be done well or very badly, and it should never be your intention to embarrass pupils or demean them in front of their peers.

Whatever you do, as a general rule, you want to avoid confrontation with pupils wherever possible. Having said that, pupils need to know that if they arrive late to their lesson, you will have a word with them or issue a warning if your school policy states this.

One of the main points to remember is never to jump to conclusions straight away. You may see a group of boys arriving two minutes late to your lesson, become irate and give them a telling-off in front of the pupils already in the class. If they then produce a note from their pastoral leader explaining a valid reason why they are late, you may look silly and have to go back on your word. It is always best to ask pupils first if they have a reason for being late. If there is no valid reason, then you can sanction them appropriately. However, the manner of speaking to pupils can vary significantly. Also, you don't always have to speak to them about being late in front of the class.

So much depends on the scenario in question. If all pupils are working silently during a starter activity and a single pupil turns up late, I would be inclined to ignore them, let them sit down and start the work. After they have sat down and got themselves sorted, I would go over to them, welcome to the lesson and then ask in almost a whisper if there was a reason for being late. If they were unable to give a valid reason, I would explain the consequence, for example that it would have to be a warning and I would write their name up on the board. The benefit of this approach is that you avoid confronting the pupil. They have not 'lost face' in front of their peers, and the calm, productive, silent starter is not interrupted. Pupils will know you have dealt with the situation without having a big song and dance about it.

If a number of pupils arrive late to your lesson and the lesson has already started, the approach may need to be different. I would ask all the pupils to wait outside the classroom and speak to them as a group. After asking them if they had a valid reason for being late, I would explain that as they were late, I would have to issue a warning (or whatever the school policy states) and then I would ask them to come in one at a time whilst writing their names up individually on the board.

You need to manage each scenario as it comes, but be prepared to send a large group of pupils out if you need to speak to them. This not only sends a message to those pupils that you won't tolerate this behaviour or lateness, but it also makes everyone else aware of it.

Top Tip: When speaking to pupils outside the classroom, always leave the door open with one foot in the classroom and one foot outside of it. This way you can have a word with pupils while also being watchful for any misbehaviour inside the lesson. Looking into the classroom a couple of times whilst speaking to the pupils outside also lets pupils inside the classroom know that you are still watching them to check they are working. **#TeachingTopTip**

WIDEN YOUR FIELD OF VIEW

Whenever possible, try to stand in the corner of your classroom. This gives you a much greater field of vision and means you can scan the whole room by only slightly turning your head. It is such an important skill, yet one that is rarely taught. If you stand in the middle of one side, or directly at the front of the classroom, you will have to turn your head 180^0 to see everyone, and there may be blind spots. By standing in a corner, you should be able to see the entire class with ease.

Taking this a step further, in my experience I have found that when pupils are on task and completing work, one of the best places to stand is in the back corner of the room. This way, you can see everyone in your classroom and can check they are working with ease. If any pupils turn around to distract or be distracted by others, you can use hand gestures to indicate they should turn around. The rest of the class will be oblivious to your instruction, and the atmosphere of your class will remain productive.

HELPING PUPILS INDIVIDUALLY

You can also use the technique of widening your viewing angle when giving pupils individual support. Always try to position yourself so that the pupil you are trying to help is between yourself and the majority of pupils in the class. By minimising the number of pupils behind your back, you maximise the possibility of spotting any off-task behaviour by others.

If, on the other hand, you position yourself so you are helping the individual pupil but have turned your back on most of the class, this is inviting trouble. Pupils could throw an object or say something, and by the time you have turned around, all pupils would be back on task and it would be impossible for you to identify the culprit/s. Pupils are clever; unless you are a step ahead of them, they will be a step ahead of you!

Top Tip: Keep a view of the whole class when helping pupils individually. When helping individual pupils, you want to ensure you maximise your field of view in relation to the class. This may involve standing on the opposite side of the pupil and looking at their work upside down. By standing and helping the pupil, you retain 'presence' over the class and can also monitor pupil behaviour. **#TeachingTopTip**

ARE YOU STUCK?

When you notice that a pupil is 'off task' or not going through the questions or work that you've asked them to do, the temptation is to tell them off straight away. This can sometimes work but it is judgemental and can often wind pupils up. It involves you jumping to conclusions, which, as I discussed in the section on dealing with late pupils, can lead to unnecessary confrontation on occasions when pupils have valid reasons. Within the classroom, I've found it's much better to pre-empt a pupil off task by asking them, 'Are you stuck?'

This simple question offers the pupil an opportunity to own up and say that they are stuck. If this is the case, then it offers you the ideal opportunity for you to sit with them and go through what you expect them to be doing.

Alternatively, if pupils reply that they are not stuck, then it gives you a great opportunity to remind them to get back to the work.

Importantly, it is a great tool to stop you firefighting, i.e. going from one pupil to another, because you can monitor the whole class during an activity. If you constantly have to move from individual to individual, you often take your eye off the whole class, who may then go off task. By asking a pupil if they're stuck, you are giving them another opportunity to get back to work without having to reprimand them, while still having the ability to watch everyone else.

It is, in effect, a way of saying 'Why aren't you working?' but in a more subtle, approachable manner.

Top Tip: **Write the time in the margin to motivate pupils where necessary.** If you have noticed that a pupil has not done as much work as you'd expect, write the exact time in the margin of their book after the last line of their work. Then tell them you will come back in a few minutes to check their progress. This usually provides them with enough of a push to knuckle down and get on with some work. When you check back, you will be able to see how much work they have done since the last time you spoke to them, and it will be much easier to hold them to account for the amount of work they've done. #TeachingTopTip

---

WHERE TO STAND AT THE BOARD

Many pupils will test you when you are teaching at the board. Most new teachers position themselves at the board as if they were writing on an ordinary piece of paper. This means standing to the side of the board (on the left if you are right-handed) with your back turned to the class. As mentioned earlier, turning your back on the class is a recipe for disaster. Pupils will be tempted to cause all sorts of havoc and you will never be able to find out who did something with 100% certainty.

When you become aware some misbehaviour is happening, you will turn around to face the pupils. But children are clever. You have given them all half a second, so by the time you are facing the class, everyone has their mouths shut, paper is on the floor and you can't tell who did what. It is a nightmare. Ok, so what should we do?

You want to spot any misbehaviour with your own eyes. The best way of doing that is by standing on the other side of the board. So, if you are right-handed, stand on the right-hand side of the board as you look at it and not the left. Reverse this if you are left-handed.

This will automatically open your body out to the whole class, as your chest will be turned towards the pupils now. In addition, try to teach with both of your feet facing the back wall of your classroom in a more open stance, so you can see most of the pupils. It will feel strange at first as it will seem like you are writing behind you, but if you can train yourself to teach like this, you will be able to control your classroom and your pupils so much better.

You can now simply turn your head if you see or hear any mischief, instead of moving your whole body. This gives you a distinct advantage and removes the half-second that pupils used to have to stop misbehaving. Surprisingly, this half-second gives the teacher a much better chance of catching any culprits. Once they realise you can identify them, pupils will soon stop doing it; they'll get bored and you'll become one of the teachers that they just can't try it on with. How unfortunate for them.

. . .

GIVING INSTRUCTIONS TO THE CLASS

Another mistake I see teachers make is getting the attention of the class before they know what they are going to do or say next. Taking the effort to stop a class in mid-activity and achieve silence takes steel and a fair bit of confidence. Some teachers do it perfectly, but then seem to get flustered by 30 pairs of eyes staring at them, expecting them to speak. Some teachers haven't remembered to 'unfreeze' the board, so need to attend to that, or they have forgotten that their computer has locked due to inactivity. So they have to log in and potentially unfreeze the screen, while the class watches and waits for their next instruction. Realistically, pupils have probably started to chat amongst themselves by now, so it takes another effort to regain their attention. But this time it will be much harder, because they'll think the teacher isn't going to say anything anyway.

To many, these scenarios may seem trivial, but with difficult classes, the five seconds it takes to solve the problem because you weren't prepared gives pupils just enough time to start conversations again, and you then need to repeat the whole process. Instead, train yourself to plan what you need to do or say next, make sure you are ready to go as soon as the class is silent and then you can start the process of gaining the pupils' attention.

Top Tip: Know what you are going to say before addressing your class. Before you address a class or interrupt their learning with a key point, always know exactly what you are going to say and how you will say it. If you are planning to go through something on the board, make sure the board is not frozen, that you are logged in, you have the correct board pen in your hand and you have checked it is working before you gain the pupils' attention. This will improve transition time and make your classroom management a whole lot easier. #TeachingTopTip

BE AWARE OF THE LIMITATIONS OF WORKING MEMORY

Numerous books have been written recently on cognitive science, which is the science behind how we learn and its role in educational pedagogy and teaching. The ideas are beyond the scope of this book, but if you are interested, I explore some of these ideas in my blog posts which you can find at www.mredwatson.com.

However, one of the key elements of cognitive science that any new teacher should know is that pupils will only be able to hold about five pieces of information in their working (short-term) memory at any one time. Giving pupils reams and reams of information is therefore futile, as it is beyond their ability to remember most of what you have just said.

One way to help pupils in your classroom is to provide new learning in small chunks, bit by bit, rather than giving them lots of information all at once. Exactly how this looks in practice in your school is likely to vary according to your school and your subject. Your departmental leader will be able to explore the finer points of pedagogy relating to your subject in more detail.

Another way to help your pupils process some of the information you have given them is to write your instructions on the board either before or after you say them. I would then keep these instructions on the board whilst pupils work through them.

This is an excellent habit to get used to because it reminds pupils of the task. You are bound to have pupils who ask you what they should be doing, even after you have told them three times. By writing up your instructions on the board, you can point to them a few times and over a few lessons and weeks, these pupils will miraculously stop asking you, as they know the work will always be projected on the board. Winner!

Top Tip: Write instructions on the board. After giving instructions to pupils, write them on the board or project them for the duration of the activity wherever possible. This will help pupils to reduce the load on their working memories whilst also stopping you having to tell pupils again and again which activities or things they should be doing. #TeachingTopTip

---

BE AWARE OF THE NOISE LEVEL

One of the best ways of assessing how well a class is working is to fine tune your listening and always keep an ear out for the class noise level. With experience, you will improve this skill over time, but if you are attuned to the noise level, you can anticipate the point at which the lifespan of your activity runs out. Make sure that you regularly take a minute to stop helping anyone and simply scan and listen. You can tell from the noise level alone whether or not pupils are on task.

Over time, you will be able to fine tune this skill to pre-empt the moment where the whole class is seemingly just having a chat because they have finished their assigned task. This will become a signal to make the transition into your next planned task. Getting the timing right takes experience, but there is no harm in starting straight away!

TIME LIMITS

One of the best pieces of advice was a little snippet I got from someone observing me early in my teaching career. They pointed out that I was using generic time limits, for example: 'we'll come back together in ten minutes' or 'we'll work on this for five minutes.' Now I didn't see anything wrong with this, but the idea they suggested struck me as genius.

Time limits such as five or ten minutes are generally used in a vague sense, so they mean nothing to pupils. They know it won't be exactly five or ten minutes.

Instead, the advice I received was to use specific time limits like four minutes or six minutes. Ultimately, it means the same thing, but the pupils will believe you are intent on watching the clock and will expect you to stop them at the appropriate point. In reality, unless you're using a timer, it will never be precisely four or six minutes, but it is a great way of giving the class a sense of urgency which can help to improve lesson productivity.

In reality, you should start or prepare to stop the task you have set pupils as soon as you hear the class starting to bubble or finishing their current task, rather than sticking to some arbitrary time limit you gave them.

Top Tip: Specific time limits. Rather than generic time limits for tasks like five or ten minutes, use specific numbers like four or seven minutes. These are also arbitrary but give pupils a much stronger impression that you are counting the minutes for the activity that they're doing and can improve lesson productivity. #TeachingTopTip

---

RESTORATIVE CONVERSATIONS

After a pupil has been sanctioned, in many schools they are often required to spend some time away from their peers in a separate classroom (often called the 'isolation room', simply 'isolation' or even 'reflection room') to act as some form of deterrent against a pupil repeating their actions. A pupil may be kept in this room for a set period of time; the specific amount of time will depend on the school's behaviour policy.

If sanctions haven't been given calmly or clearly, pupils who have been sanctioned often spend time in these rooms thinking that they have been punished for something because their teacher simply doesn't like them.

As an individual who has had to supervise pupils in these situations, where teachers have sanctioned them after having lost their patience and/or given a highly emotional rebuke of the pupil in question in front of their peers, I can understand why they may feel this way. As a result, it is important that teachers are consistent with their behaviour management policies and give sanctions clearly, concisely and unemotionally, so pupils understand they have not been sanctioned just because their teacher does not like them, but because their behaviour was not up to the required standard.

If teachers have not managed to speak to pupils they have sanctioned before they arrive at their next lesson with the teacher in question, pupils can turn up to the lesson with a mindset that their teacher dislikes them. Then, if the teacher does not meet and greet them, talk to them, or engage with them on an individual level when they enter the class, this view can be reinforced. If the situation is not managed carefully, this can lead to a negative spiral where the pupil repeats a cycle of behaviour that leads to never-ending sanctions from their teacher.

One way that can help ensure relationships are not soured is for the teacher to visit the pupil they have sanctioned as soon as possible after the lesson to talk through the incident. Through a short conversation with the pupil, there is an opportunity for pupils and teachers to talk through the event and to ensure that the slate is wiped clean before the pupil returns to their next lesson with this teacher. This should not be an opportunity for a pupil to convince a teacher to reduce or reverse a sanction. It is an opportunity for the teacher to give a fuller account of the sanction, why it was applied, and the effect the pupil's behaviour had on others in the classroom. It is also a chance for the pupil to give a fuller account of their story. Often, pupils just want to be heard and listened to, so taking the time to have the conversation will go a long way.

Importantly, teachers should never budge under any pressure from a pupil to reduce or reverse a sanction. This would be akin to scoring an own goal; it would provide a pupil with the belief that they may able to wriggle out of a similar scenario in the future. Even if you think, on reflection, that the sanction you gave was harsh, my view is that you should maintain the sanction for the pupil so they understand you are a teacher who means what they say, but you should reflect and make sure that you apply any future sanctions more consistently or fairly in line with your classroom expectations.

A phone call home to parents explaining the incident goes a long way, especially if you can pass the message to the parent before the pupil tells their one-sided account of the story. I have always found, too, that parents are often appreciative of a teacher ringing them to explain the situation. Coupled with the positive credits you've banked previously by singing their child's praises, these conversations can be very beneficial.

Nevertheless, I must stress that there are occasions where these conversations just add fuel to the fire or feel like a waste of time. Where it is apparent that a pupil has clearly done something wrong, or not met the high behavioural expectations that have been set, but that they are not going to be able to engage in a conversation about the incident, these conversations rarely work. The pupil may feel that their side of the story is 100% correct and may not be inclined to listen to the teacher's perspective at all. Where this happens, we must remember that the teacher is in charge of the classroom environment and so the teacher's account is the one that ultimately counts.

In these scenarios, I have often found that a short, sharp sentence or two can be most effective. Explaining to the pupil that the behaviour they sanctioned was not appropriate and that if repeated, would lead to the same sanction being applied consistently, then walking away from the pupil has been just as effective.

Importantly, however, the teacher must ensure that they try and repair the relationship at another time, to avoid the pupil persisting in a belief that you dislike them. If the relationship is not repaired, the pupil may enter the cycle of never-ending sanctions, which doesn't benefit anyone.

I must also stress that repairing a relationship that may have broken down as a result of a sanction you gave in a previous lesson is not necessarily an instant fix. It may take a day or a week, but I have found that pupils are remarkably forgiving if they see their teacher is taking a small interest in them.

CONSISTENCY

Following your observations (both of yourself and of others) and from reading some of the strategies above, you will have gained a greater sense of what you want your ideal classroom environment to look like. Don't worry, this doesn't have to be (and won't be) the final version of where you want to be, but it will certainly help you get your pupils closer to your expectations if you have a better idea of what you're aiming for. The key now is to be consistent in ensuring pupils follow your instructions to the letter.

Children, and adults for that matter, hate something if they think it is unfair. If there is one rule for one person, but a different rule for another, it grates with our ingrained sense of fairness. Having dealt with countless behaviour incidents across the school in my various roles, I have always found the biggest complaint from pupils who have been reprimanded or sanctioned is not about what they did or didn't do, but about the fact they got punished for it but their friend did not. This sense of unfairness is what creates their frustration, not the fact that they did something wrong in the classroom. We must try and be as consistent as possible; this certainly helps behaviour and classroom management over time.

In fact, I go as far as saying you can ask pupils to do pretty much anything you want if they know and appreciate that any sanction you apply is given consistently to all pupils in your lesson. Indeed, I once insisted upon a rule whereby they couldn't pick up anything off the floor without first asking for permission. Taken out of context, I agree this rule may seem ridiculous. Yet, through consistency of application, pupils can learn to love routines and they appreciate knowing where I stand on an issue. As long as the punishment or sanction is consistently applied 100% of the time, pupils will respect you and respect the classroom environment.

The way I see behaviour management is through the lens of trying to be an electric fence. Hear me out on this one. If you are certain that touching an electric fence will give you an electric shock, you won't touch it. If, however, if it only gives you a shock 60% of the time, therein lies a game. Sometimes I'll be hurt, and other times I won't, so 40% of the time I can get away with doing something I shouldn't. Translating this to a classroom environment, misbehaviour can arise when sanctions aren't put in place consistently.

I'd go as far as saying from my experience that some teachers will sanction a certain behaviour less than 50% of the time. This is where I see many of the problems arising in classrooms and schools. Pupils may do something against school or class rules five times in a lesson and they know the teacher spotted it but didn't sanction them. Then, on the sixth viewing, the teacher sanctions the pupil without warning and the pupil becomes irate. From the pupil's standpoint, they have been sanctioned for something they *know* the teacher has seen five times before and did nothing about. Consistency really will help you.

I've found the best teachers have a list of rules and boundaries which they are ruthlessly consistent in applying. Every lesson, every day, every year. They don't apply the rules when they're angry or fed up and relax the rules when they are having a good day. Instead, they choose a set of rules and routines and do them day in, day out, whether it's the first lesson of the term or the last lesson before Christmas. Humans like routines, but to succeed, you need to do them every day.

Top Tip: Be consistent in your application of rules. Ensure you apply your classroom rules as consistently as possible. There is nothing worse for a pupil than feeling they are being treated unfairly. By consistently applying the rules, behaviour management will improve, and pupils will know where they stand. This will make your classroom a safe, enjoyable place for pupils to learn. #TeachingTopTip

---

THE POWER OF ROUTINES

R outines are the foundation stones of behaviour and classroom management.

It's human nature to crave routine. In our daily lives, most of what we do will be an automatic routine: from brushing our teeth, driving to work, going to sleep and the way we do our shopping. It allows our brains to do these tasks subconsciously, letting us operate at a greater capacity and identify things that were previously not visible.

One of the key things for any new teacher entering the classroom is to know what routines they will adopt within their classroom and to be consistent in applying them. The most important ones are a strong entry and exit routine.

ENTRY AND EXIT ROUTINES

Can pupils enter and exit your classroom in an orderly manner? If so, pupils will see you as a calm teacher who is in control of their environment. If this is not the case, your classroom will be perceived as a place where pupils can do what they want without fear. Would you let 32 people randomly bumble in from the street into your house as they pleased? No, obviously not. So why do some teachers let their pupils do exactly that? Treat your classroom door like your own front door. You control who comes into your classroom and the manner in which they enter it. As some would say, you control the weather in your own classroom.

Your own school policy may dictate much of your class entry routine; within that, you need to find something that works for you. Something as simple as setting some work for pupils to do when they arrive will free you up to take the register and deal with any other issues. You may make pupils line up outside the classroom before they enter or allow them to come in as soon as they turn up. Either works within your school context, but it must work for you.

Importantly, the more detail that you can add in executing your desired routines, the less likelihood there is for any wriggle room for pupils when they turn up to your class.

Top Tip: Create a Do Now activity. Have some questions on the board for pupils to work on as soon as they arrive, and meet and greet pupils at the door. This allows you to control the state and manner of pupils who enter your classroom. Standing at the door also allows you to spot anyone without the correct uniform and address it there and then. I ask all pupils to fasten their top buttons and tuck their shirts in. This not only allows me to have high expectations for pupils but also makes pupils appreciate I am in control of my classroom environment.

What if a pupil refuses? Well, if they won't do up their top button or tuck their shirt in, are they going to follow your classroom rules inside the classroom? Exactly, they're not. So why let them inside in the first place? What you end up finding out is that if you do it religiously enough, you will see pupils tidying their uniform as they walk down the corridor on the way to your lessons. #TeachingTopTip

---

Now, before I create a cohort of maverick teachers, whatever you do must fit within your own school policy. If not, it won't work and may be picked up.

Like anything, instilling a routine like this takes a lot of work at the beginning but is well worth the effort over time. Routines take time, lots of time. Don't think that because pupils did it once, they will do it like that all the time. In fact, I've found that routines can take up to three months to become fully automatic, perhaps even longer in some cases. So, the key is to ensure the routine is done correctly every time and that pupils are sanctioned if they disregard it.

To set a routine, you must repeat the expected actions tens of times. It is not enough to do it well half a dozen times and expect them to do it. Over time, unless you check it is being done exactly as you wish, before you know it the routine you spent so long creating has vanished.

For an exit routine, I would ensure all pupils stand behind their chairs in silence and are dismissed one row at a time. This ensures that pupils are calm before they leave your classroom and you can see that any paper or items on the floor are picked up, tables and chairs are aligned perfectly, and pupils can make an orderly exit from your lesson.

There are myriad variations of this, but the key is to find

something that works for you and to stick with it. Repeat it until it becomes automatic for you and for the pupils, and have the routine written down and planned in as much detail as you possibly can.

I've had classes that have become so good at their packing away routine that I have given them an option to come up with a 'code-word'; as soon as I have said it, pupils have packed away in silence. With practice, I've found a class can pack away within 30 seconds. This takes practice and you won't get there straight away, but it certainly shows the power of routines within a classroom and the learning benefits that this can provide.

Entry and exit routines are the most important in my eyes, but you don't need to stop there. The following routines, some of which I cover in this book, are also worth considering:

- Presentation of books
- Glue sticks
- Homework
- Register
- Pupils arriving late
- Partner work
- Group work
- Any others you think will help.

The key is to make these automatic, allowing you to free up your mental capacity to deal with any other problems that may arise within the lesson. Dealing with behaviour management whilst also expecting pupils to pack away without a set routine is a recipe for chaos, whereas if you know exactly how pupils are going to pack away, you will spot that Jack at the back is about to climb out of a window.

BE EXPLICIT

Following on from routines in your lesson, be explicit about you want. The clearer your instructions, the more likely it is for pupils to follow what you are saying. Asking pupils to simply 'Pack away' is a recipe for disaster. They will invent 30 different versions of what 'packing away' entails. It is far more efficient to have one clear version of packing away and ask them to do it explicitly. State what you want and insist that they carry it out. If they do not do it precisely the way you asked, make them do it again. The hardest part is the beginning. You must then follow it through consistently.

When starting a routine, it is also useful to break the actions down into one instruction at a time. If your overall packing away routine has ten instructions in it, you will not be able to list all ten and expect your pupils to start straight away. It won't work. Instead, issue one instruction and ask them to do it. If they have done it well, move onto instruction two. However, if instruction one was not done to your standard, get them to do it again and again and again until they understand what your standards are.

This will take time. Pupils will think you are just doing it for one lesson and that you will have forgotten by tomorrow. Get your pupils to practise your routine repeatedly, so they know you are serious about it. Routines support good behaviour in the classroom and they also increase the learning time, helping you to maximise pupil outcomes.

You should also be explicit about the standard of presentation and quality of work you expect in pupils' exercise books. An individual's exercise book can tell you a surprising amount about their attitude to learning.

. . .

EXERCISE BOOKS

The way pupils present their work is a reflection of the pride that they take in their teacher, their subject and their studies. Like it or not, school leaders will probably use your pupils' books as a proxy for the quality of education that you are delivering as a teacher in your school.

I have some top tips to help you ensure your pupils' books are the best in the school. The quality of teaching and learning is much more important than book presentation, but in my experience, the two often go hand in hand. On the whole, the best schools and the best teachers I've seen also have the best books. Books do seem to be the best proxy for learning when assessing teacher performance in the classroom.

When you take on a new class, the important thing is to be explicit with what you expect a 'good book' to look like. I would physically show them: use a visualiser or create a slide to show them what your expectations are. This is the start. Simply showing them will result in some pupils doing exactly what you ask and others not following it as you'd wish. The best way to combat poor presentation is to correct it 'in the moment' by circulating the classroom whilst you teach.

As a teacher, you will be constrained or assisted by your school policy in terms of what sanctions or rewards you can offer for the presentation of work. But you don't need rewards or sanctions to support your high expectations. Going around with your marking pen and simply ticking pages that are presented well will give pupils the positivity to continue presenting work as you wish.

If doodling or graffiti appears in pupils' books, circling it at the time is the most effective form of stopping this from appearing in your books. Physically walking around the room checking that pupils have underlined their dates and titles is also an important aspect. Writing a comment two weeks after a pupil has drawn some graffiti is less useful, akin to telling off a toddler for something they did two weeks ago.

Experience will tell you that the best time to set expectations of books is in the first week or even the very first lesson. You need to load your effort massively into books as soon as you start teaching your class. Leaving it a few weeks before checking will lead to some catastrophic books that look like they have been put through a washing machine.

Although it may be slightly more time-consuming, whenever I have a new class, after the first or second lesson I get all the pupil books in and sort them into two piles: good and bad. I hand back the good books with praise; I set aside the bad books to hand out personally so I can tell each pupil how they need to improve and re-set my expectations. This immediately conveys to your pupils the standards and high expectations that you have of them, and it will save you an inordinate amount of time reminding them in the long run.

You will probably have a prescriptive marking policy at your school. This is not only an opportunity to mark their work but also a chance to re-set your standards of presentation. I have always found comments at the end of a piece of work to be much less effective than telling pupils what they need to improve in person, but again you will be constrained by your school policy.

Regarding presentation, I always look at my books with a pad of sticky notes next to me. If any pupil needs to improve their presentation, I put a sticky note summarising the problem on the front of their book and put it in a separate pile. After completing the marking, I will have one pile of books that are excellent and another with sticky notes on them. Initially, the pile of books with notes on may be quite high, but the fact that you identify them and engage in individual conversations with pupils about their presentation means that each time you mark their work, there will be fewer and fewer.

When handing the books out, those with sticky notes will require you to talk with each pupil individually (often no more than about 10 seconds each), telling them exactly what you liked and what they need to improve. It may be comments such as all your dates and titles need underlining, there is doodling in your book which is unacceptable, you have drawn diagrams in pen not pencil, you have incomplete details on the front of your book, or you're writing in green but you need to write in black/blue pen. These are just examples; you will have your own bugbears in the classroom.

Top Tip: When marking books, attach a sticky note to the front of the books summarising the particular points that need improving. Place these books in a separate pile and speak to these pupils individually when handing out the class books. From experience, I have found that this is far more impactful than writing comments in their books. Just remember to take off the sticky note yourself and put it in the bin, otherwise you will end up with lots of notes covering your floor! #TeachingTopTip

---

Because books are used to assess the quality of learning in your classroom, it pays dividends to make sure that pupils are presenting their work nicely. Before you start your first school, move to a new school, or start with a new class, remember to state your expectations clearly, so pupils are aware of exactly what you are looking for.

TRANSITIONS

Transitioning between tasks occurs frequently within each lesson. If you can make your transitions tight, moving from one task to another with minimal disruption, you will have expert control of your class and your pupils will benefit enormously from the time it frees up for additional learning.

Conversely, if transitions are clunky, slow and inefficient, you will start to lose control and pupils will get the impression you don't know what you're doing. If they think you are making the lesson up as you go, they are likely to start acting up in between activities. Then you will find yourself expending a lot of energy to stop and start the class, as you try to make pupils settle down and start their new activity.

Example scenario: You are teaching at the whiteboard at the front of the classroom and the next activity you want pupils to do is to complete a worksheet you have printed for them. How can you make the transition as smooth as possible?

Option 1) You finish teaching and then hand out 32 individual worksheets to each pupil. This option takes a lot of time and gives pupils the opportunity to talk and be 'off task'. By the time you have handed all the sheets out, the chances are pupils will be disengaged and you will need to call the class back together again before starting the activity.

Option 2) You finish teaching and then hand piles of the worksheet to the pupils at the end of each row who can then pass them along when requested. This approach means you hand the papers out to fewer people, can manage the class better and reduce the time in between activities, which is often referred to as 'dead' time. This process can become part of a classroom routine in which you can train your pupils to become proficient. It has been known for pupils to hand out all worksheets to their peers in a matter of seconds using this system.

Option 3) The method I personally favour, however, is handing out worksheets in piles at the end of the row (face down so pupils aren't tempted to look) during the starter or previous activity. When you finish teaching at the board, you can ask pupils to hand out the sheets to others in their row. This saves a lot of time and means pupils have less time to become disengaged. You can still observe the class to check they remain 'on task'; in the long term you will save a significant amount of time which you can allocate for additional learning, whilst still maintaining super control of your classroom.

How can you teach yourself to do this? Always be conscious of the activity coming up next. When planning your lesson, you should have already worked out the structure and activities required. However, the way that worked best for me was to train myself to recall what I wanted the pupils to do after I had stopped a class and finished speaking to them. If it required them to do a worksheet, I'd hand them out before I spoke. If they needed glue sticks, rulers, pencils, compasses or colouring pencils, I handed them out before I spoke. As soon as I'd issued an instruction to the class, the pupils already had what they needed in front of them.

Making this process automatic takes time and experience, but you can easily train yourself to think in this way. In a short space of time, you will find your classroom management and control of your class soar.

Top Tip: Make your transitions as smooth as possible.
Train yourself to think about what activity you want
pupils to complete after you have finished speaking to
them. Make it a habit to hand out any key materials and
resources to pupils at the ends of each row before you
stop a class and issue an instruction. This will save 'dead'
time and ensure you maximise learning moments in your
lessons. #TeachingTopTip

4

PEDAGOGY

When starting out as a teacher, not only do you have to worry about controlling the class and trying to get them to work as you want, but you must also try to teach them. This may sound simple, but in the early days of your teaching career you will probably be happy if a lesson goes without a hiccup and no one has been told off. Over time, you will realise that behaviour management is only part of the standards you are expected to fulfil. Your top priority is to teach pupils, not just be their childminder for the duration of a lesson.

As the teacher, it is very important to remember that you are the expert and pupils are the novices. It is hard for teachers to appreciate how little pupils actually know; this is sometimes called the 'curse of knowledge'. It arises from the fact that when an individual gains knowledge, it is very hard for that individual to appreciate how someone else doesn't know as much as they do. This happens in all walks of life, but it is particularly pertinent to teachers, especially early in their careers. What may seem mundane, straight-forward, or common sense to a teacher fresh from university is likely to be knowledge that your pupils surprisingly don't have, and the lack of it will hinder them in their future learning. This is where subject pedagogy plays a huge part in building expertise as a teacher.

Put simply, pedagogy is the practice of how to teach. It concerns the nuances of how to model, explain and deliver topics to pupils in the best possible way that enables them to understand the material you are presenting. Most of the highest attaining pupils in your classes will manage to pick up a topic without a fantastic explanation. These pupils may even be able to teach themselves if they are working from a textbook or other resource given to them, or if they have the independence to revise and teach themselves when they go home.

However, I have always found that effective pedagogy supports the weakest pupils the best. With strong pedagogy, by benefiting the lowest attaining pupils in your class, you will improve the learning of the whole class. Explaining topics clearly is the bread and butter of any strong practitioner.

USE YOUR COLLEAGUES

Before you teach a topic to a class, utilise your network of departmental colleagues to identify different ways of teaching that topic. Be humble. The way you would tackle a question or a topic may work for you personally, as an expert, but it may not be the best way of introducing the topic to pupils for the very first time. Your preferred way may come from having developed your thinking over years of practice, but it is likely to be more difficult for the pupils to understand. Your new challenge is to introduce a concept to pupils when you have never done it before. The best people to ask for advice on this are your department colleagues. They will want to help you because it is such a critical part of teaching.

If you are trying to take shortcuts when planning your lessons, failing to practise your explanations before you teach pupils, or avoiding asking colleagues for advice, you will be found out. When you start as a teacher, there is a wealth of pedagogy that you will not have been exposed to, even during your Initial Teacher Training (ITT). Within your ITT, you will focus on aspects of pedagogy and delivery, but this will not cover every topic across your subject curriculum. It is certainly not likely to cover every topic in the level of depth that is required to become expert at teaching it to your pupils.

It takes time, even years, to develop a strong grasp of the best way to teach certain topics to different groups of pupils. Ask colleagues how to teach the topics that are coming up for you to deliver. If you don't, you will pay the price, as pupils will not understand what you are teaching them. This will knock their confidence in you as a teacher, may result in increasing behaviour problems in the class, and will result in far more time and effort than if you had researched the best approach for a topic beforehand.

That said, even if you teach the topic or introduce the content in a way that you have practised and discussed with colleagues, it may still go wrong. Yet you will have done everything possible to make sure the lesson goes as smoothly as possible. You can reflect on this yourself (question yourself, replay the scenario again mentally, imagine what would happen if you did something differently) to work out why the lesson did not go as well as planned.

Once you have discussed the best method to introduce a topic to a class, it's helpful to do a trial run through (ideally on the actual whiteboard you will be teaching on), to rehearse how you will introduce it physically and verbally using the board. This will ensure you are aware of the trickiest points of the explanation including how to draw or label certain elements. It will reduce your nerves when you introduce it to the class for the first time and will lead to rapid improvements in your teaching practice. While it may seem unfamiliar for new teachers to do this, especially in an empty classroom with no pupils, we are aiming for excellence and practising the small constituent parts of teaching will accelerate your progress.

It would be even better, although nerve-wracking at first, to get your mentor or a colleague to film you teaching it. By watching it back and reflecting on your delivery, you will make exponential gains and be a superstar teacher before you even know it (even if you do cringe slightly at the sound of your own voice at first!). You will spot elements that you know could be improved, and because you have seen them at first hand, you will be the best person to correct them.

Not everyone will do this. Some new teachers may be happy to rock up, do a day's teaching and go home at the end of the day. But you're not one of those teachers. The very fact you're reading this book means you're someone who knows teaching is going to be difficult but who is looking for the strategies to become an excellent teacher, fast. For that, I salute you. You will stand out from the crowd, for all the best reasons.

In pedagogy, it is easy for a teacher to walk into a room to observe an expert teacher and think it all looks so straightforward, with perfect explanations, delivery and examples. Trust me, they have perfected their craft. They did not teach like that on day one. Talk to them. Question them. Observe them. Find out what they do that makes it look easy. Even if they don't think they have the answers, speaking to them will offer you new insights into how they do what they do. There will be things you can take away from them that you can incorporate into your own practice to improve yourself as a teacher.

Top Tip: Ask colleagues how to teach topics before you teach them to pupils. Use the expertise of colleagues to explain the best way of teaching topics to pupils. The art of effective pedagogy takes years to develop, so shorten the process by asking colleagues first. This will give you a better chance of pupils understanding what you are trying to teach them. #TeachingTopTip

---

DIFFERENTIATION

Differentiation is a commonly used word in education that means ensuring that the task you have set is suitable for every learner in your classroom. It is commonly discussed at length in teacher training courses across the country and seems to have morphed into many different meanings, some of which can, in my opinion, be quite damaging to pupils in classrooms.

Some have twisted the definition to imply that you need to plan thirty individual variations of a task, personalised to each pupil. This is clearly impractical. I would argue that every child is different, but they don't all need their own specific variation of an individual task. It is unnecessary and results in an inadequate interpretation of what good differentiation is in the classroom.

Others have not gone quite so far and instead propose three different levels of worksheets for high, middle, and low attaining pupils. This may involve having Bronze (easiest questions), Silver (middle questions) and Gold (hardest questions). Again, this requires additional work for teachers and if not done correctly, will create low expectations of pupils. If you label pupils in this way, it means not all pupils work through all the questions, so you are automatically creating a difference between the highest and lowest attaining pupils in the class. By default, the lower attaining pupils will never manage to catch up with the higher attaining pupils, as they are potentially always doing easier work! The gap between the two groups is only likely to diverge further, making it even harder to ensure everyone is working to the level that is required of them. This is differentiation gone wrong. Unfortunately and alarmingly, it still exists in schools and is still being taught in some teacher training courses. Beware.

A far better method of differentiation is to give everyone the same task. Here, you have high expectations for all. The standard of work you set is the standard for all learners, regardless of their starting point. You should then see differentiation as scaffolding (similar to that used to build a skyscraper). Scaffolding is only ever used to build something that couldn't have been built without it. Otherwise, what is the point?

So, once you have given everyone a task, you should see who is doing well with it and who needs extra support. With the pupils who need extra support, you can then give them a pre-prepared scaffolded sheet for the same activity or differentiate according to the time you give to individual pupils. This is a much better approach to help all pupils excel; it also saves on workload by removing the need to produce lots of different tasks, which only further entrench disadvantage. Everyone should be able to access the work and you achieve differentiation through the support or time you offer pupils in achieving the same standard of work as their peers in the classroom.

Finally, if you give a pupil a scaffolded sheet, don't forget to take it away when they no longer need it. Remember, scaffolding is only ever needed while a building is in progress. Once it has been built, you don't keep the scaffolding there, you remove it, as you don't need it anymore!

Top Tip: Differentiation. Differentiation is like scaffolding. Use it only where it is necessary and don't give separate tasks to separate groups of pupils. Instead, have one task and scaffold support into that activity. This could be a scaffolding sheet you prepare beforehand or extra time given to pupils who are struggling with the activity. **#TeachingTopTip**

QUESTIONING

Questioning is one of the key aspects of effective pedagogy. How do you know that pupils have understood a topic? Asking, 'Do you understand this?' is not an effective means of questioning.

A good technique to use when questioning a class is to pose a question and then state the name at the end of the question after a slight pause, giving considerable 'wait time'. That way, all pupils in your class will think of the answer before you ask one individual for their response. If you put the name first and then ask the question, some of the other pupils will switch off and lose concentration; they know they are not going to be asked for their response. For example, 'What is the capital of England.....Ben?' is much better than 'Ben, what is the capital of England?' In the second example, only Ben needs to concentrate as he is the one being asked. In the first example, every pupil in the class needs to be ready to answer and the 'wait time' before the teacher states the child's name provides time for every pupil in the classroom to think of their answer first.

You can also target your questions to certain individuals. Certain schools may have a policy of prioritising pupils for questioning to compensate for their disadvantage or lack of academic progress.

In addition, you could make it common practice to question your weakest pupils regularly in lessons. There is always a temptation to ask the pupils who you know will give you the right answer. It is human nature. You are slightly nervous, teaching in front of 32 pupils, and there are twenty blank faces all staring at you. You pose a question and ask the best pupil in the class. They, of course, give you the correct answer, but on starting the activity you soon realise that hardly anyone else knows what they are doing.

It is often much better practice to question some of the weakest pupils. If they can give you a detailed response which shows clear understanding, you can be more confident that the rest of the class will also understand.

Top Tip: Get used to asking some of the weakest pupils in the class. If they understand it, you can be more confident that the rest have understood it. **#TeachingTopTip**

Another strategy that can be used when pupils are stuck answering a question, is to ask more questions. Although this may seem counter-intuitive, through further questioning, pupils can become "unstuck" as you can tease the right answer out of them. As a result, the pupil's confidence grows, as they know they have not had to rely on another pupil to provide the answer for them.

The final questioning strategy that can be extremely effective is not asking pupils to put their hands up to respond to a question. By having a 'no hands up' rule within your classroom, you ensure that you engage all learners all of the time. You can choose pupils at random or you can target your questioning to certain individuals, rather than always asking those who volunteer their responses. By only choosing individuals who raise their hands, certain pupils may relax and not give their full attention as they know they may never be called upon by the teacher to answer any questions. A 'no hands up' rule prevents this from happening and can transform the engagement and attention of pupils within your classroom.

Top Tip: '**No hands up**.' Introduce a 'no hands up' rule in your classroom. By choosing to question certain pupils deliberately, rather than choosing pupils who volunteer responses by raising their hand, you increase the engagement and learning within your classroom. **#TeachingTopTip**

HOW TO BALANCE EFFORT WITH IMPACT

Many initial teacher training (ITT) providers recommend using a variety of activities to engage learners and to stimulate their learning. This may include creating card-sorts, treasure hunts (where pupils are out of their seats going from one clue to the other) and tarsias (similar to educational dominoes where questions and answers all join together to make one big shape), amongst other things.

These activities may have a time and a place, but the key thing to remember is never to mistake activity for achievement. Just because 30 pupils are making a lot of noise walking around the classroom looking for their next clue doesn't mean they are learning anything. A teacher's job is to ensure pupils are learning. Recent research in cognitive science explains that we remember what we think about or attend to. As a teacher, you should ask yourself 'what are my pupils going to be thinking about or attending to during this activity?'

A lesson spent making revision posters may be planned with the best of intentions, but I would argue pupils will spend most of the lesson thinking about what colours to use, what border to use and whether to use their favourite gel pens, rather than concentrating on any of the material the teacher wanted them to revise. With treasure hunts, what percentage of the time are pupils likely to be thinking about the learning the teacher wants them to focus on? And how much of the time will they spend walking around the classroom, having conversations with their peers?

Top Tip: When planning activities, focus on what you want pupils to think about. We remember what we think about, so design your activities with this in mind. If your pupils will spend more time wandering about, colouring, or sticking something in, ask yourself if it is the best use of their time. Never mistake activity for achievement. #TeachingTopTip

---

At the risk of sounding like a fun sponge, I'm sure these activities are designed to stimulate some interest, enthusiasm and love for the subject, but it is also worth asking yourself whether the pupils are actually learning. If the answer is no, evaluate the impact of the activity.

You also need to consider the effort that it takes to create, produce and deliver the activity. Creating a card sort, placing them in envelopes, making sure pupils return the cards to the envelopes and collecting them back in takes time and effort. What happens if a pupil loses one of the cards? Can you use it again? If not, are you going to go through all the envelopes to check they're all complete sets?

These are all questions you need to ask yourself before you rush into producing these activities. A good benchmark is that the time taken to produce the activity should never be more than the time taken for pupils to complete it. If it takes you an hour to create a card sort, but it only takes the pupils ten minutes to do it, was that an effective use of your time? I'd argue it's not. The only caveat is that it might be worth it eventually if you laminate the cards to make them sturdy, have impeccable behaviour management skills so can ensure all cards go back in the correct envelopes and you re-use the task several times throughout the course of your teaching career.

Top Tip: Never spend more time creating an activity than it will take pupils to complete it. #TeachingTopTip

---

LESSONS ARE THE WRONG UNIT OF TIME

When you plan your lessons, one of the key pieces of advice I can give to you is to plan a sequence of lessons rather than individual lessons. Learning outcomes are broad and take time. Planning lessons in sequences will also save you a considerable amount of time, as you can appreciate where the pupils are coming from and also where they need to get to. You should not regard a lesson as a three-course meal with a starter, a main and a dessert. Instead, see it as one piece of a larger sequence within your teaching plan.

Also, by planning the sequence of lessons, you are much better prepared to go through content at the pace required by the pupils. If pupils grasp concepts easily, you are able to move on and vice versa. Without adequate planning, however, if pupils finish what you had planned for an individual lesson early, you will be standing at the front of your class hoping that time will speed up until you hear the sound of the bell for the next lesson to start. This is also an important concept to remember when you are asked to do lesson plans for observations during your training years; you don't have to teach everything on your plan within a single lesson.

Many new and inexperienced teachers, when asked to create a lesson plan, mistakenly believe that they need to teach everything in the plan within the lesson for it to be a 'good lesson'. This is a myth. Experience tells you that learning is complex and doesn't fit into neat, discrete, lesson sized blocks. Instead, one piece of work may take less time than you were expecting, so you complete content more quickly than you expected. Conversely, some learning will take much longer and the lesson sequence will need to be prolonged. This is good, responsive teaching in action. It is the hallmark of a good teacher. Do not feel that you have failed because you have not stuck rigidly to the lesson plan you originally created. It's quite the opposite: you are learning to adapt to the needs of your pupils within their learning journey.

Top Tip: Plan lesson sequences, not individual lessons. Planning a sequence of lessons will help plan the progression of learning towards a pre-determined end point. It will save time, will help structure the lessons and will also enable you to be more responsive to the learning needs of your pupils as they arise. **#TeachingTopTip**

THE CURSE OF POWERPOINT ANIMATIONS

You're new to teaching and you want to impress your pupils by having the best slides in town. You stay awake for hours perfecting the animations which fly in from all corners of the screen. What's the point? Pupils won't appreciate it and it is a drain on your time.

Instead, apply your effort to the things that matter. Use your time perfecting how to deliver content to classes, your explanations and the questions you're going to ask. These are far more valuable things to focus on than making sure your slide animations are excellent.

It is a mistake that many teachers make, and it is not impactful at all. When training, I heard many horror stories of teachers staying up late perfecting their slides. It's a waste of time; don't fall into this trap.

Top Tip: Avoid animating your PowerPoint slides. Use animations sparingly for when they are essential, not for making your PowerPoint a work of art. The effort they take to do compared to the impact that they have in your lesson is minimal. Your time is better spent perfecting your pedagogy. **#TeachingTopTip**

FIND OUT THE TEACHING SHORTCUTS

Teachers are busy people. In addition to a full teaching timetable, teachers are expected to call parents, mark work and plan lessons, amongst a host of other tasks varying in complexity. All of these responsibilities place differing demands on yourself and compete for your time. Often, you may find yourself with too much to do in the time available for their completion. Therefore, you need to find shortcuts.

One of the classic mistakes new teachers make is to do everything to perfection, 100% of the time. Before long, you wonder how other teachers cope with the enormous volume of work handed to them by senior leaders. Admittedly, your colleagues may have more experience, so it will take them less time to complete certain tasks. Even so, you look on with admiration at how they do it all when it takes you so long.

Now, let me let you into a secret. They are probably finding shortcuts. These shortcuts aren't reducing the quality of their work, but they are ensuring teachers stay sane and are fresh and ready to teach the following day.

Each school and department will have their own shortcuts and you will need to ask around to use the experience and wisdom of others to find out what these are for your individual school.

Some examples may involve navigating your school marking policy, ensuring it takes you less time to mark books whilst still retaining the impact that marking work will have. This may include moving towards whole class marking, where you identify the trends for the whole class and provide feedback as a group rather than to individual pupils. Often, the comments that teachers make for each pupil are remarkably similar; whole class feedback prevents you having to write the same comment in every book. If you are considering doing this, just be sure it fits within your school and/or departmental policies.

There will be other shortcuts that your colleagues have found which don't reduce the impact of their work. Ask colleagues what they are; they will be more than happy to share their ideas.

Some other ideas that may work, depending on your school context, are introducing a coded marking scheme. This can be used to save a teacher having to write in full sentences each time. For example, writing 'sp.' next to a spelling mistake as opposed to writing 'spelling' will save you a lot of time when marking a class set of books. You can find lots of shortcuts like this.

Another simple suggestion is to ask pupils to hand their books in open at their last piece of work when you collect pupil books for marking. This may again seem trivial, but finding the correct page in 32 books can take a considerable amount of time. Coupled with a coded, or whole class marking process, you will find the time savings add up significantly.

Where appropriate, and admittedly this may depend on your subject, you could also ask pupils to self-mark their own work. Use this approach with caution, as it is open to abuse by pupils if they are not properly trained, but if done well, it means you don't need to mark their work. Instead, as a teacher, you can check that they have checked their work. It will increase the time available for you to help rectify any mistakes or misconceptions that may arise within the classroom.

Increasingly, schools are using visualisers in the classroom for teachers to mark a piece of work in front of a class. As the teacher marks it at the front of the class, pupils will be able to identify whether they have written something similar or used similar bits of knowledge in their answer. This feedback can be instant, which can be significantly more effective than getting their books two weeks after they have completed the work. I would argue it is also much more effective.

Other strategies include asking pupils to stick sheets or feedback labels in their books before you collect them in. I have seen teachers spend significant amounts of their own time after school has closed for the day sticking sheets into pupils' books. When questioned on this, they argue it is necessary to keep their books immaculate. I agree it is important that pupils present their work well, but I completely disagree that pupils are incapable of doing it themselves. We have already spoken in the previous chapter about setting routines for pupils to follow. A 'sticking in' routine may sound patronising and childish, but it may be necessary. You will be surprised at how poorly some pupils can do it, but I would argue that with practice, pupils can be trained to follow your high expectations, saving you from having to do it yourself.

The strategies I have mentioned here are not exhaustive, and there will be countless timesaving activities that you should take advantage of. Of course, make sure you are doing what is expected of you according to your school and departmental policies, but look for ways to shorten the process without impacting on pupil outcomes.

Top Tip: Teaching shortcuts. Ask colleagues and look out for timesaving hacks that will mean you can spend less effort whilst maximising impact. This will free you up to spend your time in other areas. **#TeachingTopTip**

THE CURSE OF SHOWBIZ LESSONS

The 'showbiz' lesson; what a waste of time. I know teachers enter the profession to engage and inspire pupils in their subject, but we must not forget the reason we are in front of the classroom: for pupils to learn. Trying to make lessons fun and engaging may sound exciting, but it requires significant amounts of energy and often doesn't lead to optimal learning.

Years later, pupils often remember the 'fun lesson' but cannot recall the actual learning that was supposed to take place. Showbiz lessons can help build excitement and relationships with your pupils, but they should not be regarded as the gold standard of teaching. Excellent teaching is where pupils learn, and this should always be the focus.

There may be a time and a place for eating an orange whilst doing a handstand to demonstrate the digestion process, but the opportunities are few and far between, so I advise caution in choosing when to use these lessons, if at all. Pupils are in school to learn, not to be entertained.

However, if you are a teacher that can engage learners doing something extraordinary whilst also ensuring they are learning, then I applaud you. Please get in touch and I would love to come and watch you teach!

My view is that pupils enjoy learning. Everyone does. I believe that the joy of learning comes from the learning itself rather than simply being entertained. If pupils can see that their teacher is teaching them something and understand that they are learning, then the rest follows. You will create a positive feedback loop where learning creates further learning which in turn builds success later in their journeys.

Top Tip: Never mistake activity for achievement. Just because the classroom looks hectic and pupils are running around trying to find clues for a treasure hunt you spent six hours creating doesn't mean they are learning anything. **#TeachingTopTip**

BUILD YOUR PEDAGOGICAL KNOWLEDGE

It is important that as a teacher, regardless of your level of experience, you keep searching for improvements in your practice. There will always be new ideas about how to model and explain certain topics to pupils. Fresh approaches to how pupils learn may emerge as a result of advancements in science and learning. It is for this reason that teachers must be constantly engaged with the latest developments in their subject discipline. Investing in yourself as a teacher is crucial and will be discussed within the next chapter.

GENERAL ADVICE

By reading this book, you are committed to investing in yourself and becoming the best teacher you can be in the shortest possible time frame. For that reason, I am sure you will be an excellent listener and will take feedback in your stride in order to improve. For some, however, this may be more of a challenge. Depending on your own personal context and the level of experience you bring to the profession, you may or may not take to the teaching profession easily. This is totally understandable.

For some new teachers, it will be the first time they have struggled at anything. You may have excelled at school yourself, been to a prestigious university and graduated with a first-class degree. Yet once you enter your first classroom, all of this means nothing to the pupils in front of you.

Some teachers may find it difficult to acclimatise to this unfamiliar environment and may not feel comfortable being told that there are a lot of things they need to improve. Be prepared for that, and face the challenge head on. Teaching is a wonderful profession and like anything, the more you practise and improve, the better you will become.

The best approach for all teachers new to the profession, however, is to be humble. Humility goes a long way.

BE PROFESSIONAL

BE HUMBLE

As a new teacher, you have a lot to learn. However confident you are in your abilities, learn to appreciate that people offering feedback are only trying to help. Listen to everything. Try everything they suggest, at least once.

Appreciate that any feedback you receive is coming from a good place and that everyone is working towards the same thing: the best learning for the pupils in your classroom. People want to support you and help you be the best. Feedback can hurt sometimes, as you are putting your heart and soul into what you do, but you must trust that it is done with the best of intentions.

Be a sponge. Teaching is tough but many of the problems you face will not be new. Colleagues and mentors are likely to have experienced what you are going through, so use them to help you maximise your progress towards being an excellent teacher. They will be aware of the pitfalls, challenges and obstacles that will be in your way and will have the knowledge to guide you. Ask questions and spend time with them to use their knowledge and wisdom to your advantage. There is also a wealth of information on Twitter, in blogs and in conferences, to support you in improving your knowledge, understanding and development. This will all enable you to accelerate your progress within the profession.

. . .

BE A ROLE MODEL

Teaching is a privilege, allowing you to impart knowledge and advice to countless pupils during your career. You have the opportunity to instil a love of your subject in the pupils you teach and ensure that they develop the skills and knowledge to give themselves the greatest chance of success in the future.

With this privilege, however, comes responsibility.

As teachers, we hold a position of public authority, responsibility and trust and therefore need to act accordingly. Within schools, teachers are 'in loco parentis', which translates as 'in the place of a parent'. We are responsible for not only the education of a child but also their safety and wellbeing while in our care. Pupils will look up to us as respected adults and will model many of their behaviours on us.

Not only is it important to act as a role model within the school grounds, but it is also sensible to bear this in mind outside of the school premises too. In fact, it is the second main constituent of the Teachers' Standards which we must all follow. The first part of the Teachers' Standards is related to 'Teaching' and the second part concerns 'Personal and Professional Conduct', which relates to conduct inside and outside of school.

In any profession there will be individuals who behave inappropriately and cause reputational harm to their employer and themselves. Within teaching, I would argue that the level of responsibility is greater, based on the extent of the role we play within society.

Everyone will make their own mind up about what is appropriate and inappropriate, and who am I to judge? But it is worth noting that any behaviour outside school that is inappropriate may require action from your school headteacher if they are made aware of what has happened.

Clearly, you may hope that your school headteacher may never find out, but you would be surprised at what can happen. Some of the examples I am about to give may illustrate how information can be obtained from a wide range of sources.

Top Tip: Be responsible for your actions. As teachers, we are in privileged and respected positions. With this privilege comes responsibility. Think carefully about your conduct and behaviour outside of the school gates. At one end of the spectrum, your behaviour may bring embarrassment upon yourself, which will make your job more difficult in school. At the other end, your employer may have to take disciplinary action against you. **#TeachingTopTip**

I offer the following examples not in a judgemental sense, but as a reminder that any of our behaviour may be spotted, noted and passed on, which can lead to embarrassment, or more extreme disciplinary action if required.

Example 1:

A colleague I know who was in their early teaching career was on a famous dating app that involved swiping left or right to identify a 'match.' This app was hugely popular and used by millions of people, so it was hardly a surprise that teachers were using it. However, the teacher's profile was found on the app and their use of it became well known amongst pupils. The teacher was mortified and found it difficult to carry on teaching as normal. She was highly embarrassed, having been completely unaware that using the app could have caused such problems in school.

Teachers will obviously continue to use apps like this, but they should be mindful of the potential unintended consequences. If you do use one, check that the settings are configured as tightly as possible to reduce the likelihood of this happening to you.

Example 2:

In my first year of teaching, I attended the staff Christmas meal and one member of staff got so drunk they threw a wine glass over their shoulder on the way out of the venue. The glass shattered, and the teacher continued to walk away as if nothing had happened. Now whether you think it is acceptable or not, the teacher in question was in a highly responsible position and even though it may have been behind closed doors, it affected their reputation. People don't forget.

If you are ever in a similar situation, you will not want to be the talk of the staff room the following day. Not only could it land you in trouble, damage your reference and affect future promotion opportunities, but it could also make your life very uncomfortable in school.

At school events, you will often find that headteachers show their face at the events for only a short time. They will often arrive, buy a few drinks, have a few conversations and then go home. This is not because headteachers don't like to socialise and talk to colleagues; far from it. In fact, they are doing it for a couple of reasons. Firstly, they appreciate that colleagues may not be able to relax and enjoy themselves if their boss is present, because they may feel they are being judged. Secondly, headteachers are protecting themselves from having to make any uncomfortable decisions the following day or week if any members of staff act inappropriately.

Example 3:

I know a teacher who claimed that they were attending

their grandfather's funeral, when in reality they were attending the first day of the Glastonbury music festival. If teachers lie to their employers about attending an event like this, they are putting themselves at substantial risk. If the individual is spotted on television or is identifiable from a photo, they are taking a chance that their employer or someone connected to the school won't see it. It only takes one individual to inform the headteacher of their presence for it to become a serious disciplinary issue. You may think the chances of this are slim, but it does not take much for anyone to be found out.

Example 4:

I know of a teacher who got drunk while travelling to a rugby match by train and started to share information about the school and some pupils. A passenger, who was not associated with the individual but was also a teacher, overheard the conversation and was appalled. They took notes, called the teacher's school the following Monday, and reported that member of staff to the school principal.

Don't get me wrong; we should be able to have a good time and enjoy ourselves, but we have to remember we are in a position of public responsibility. You don't want to give anyone any ammunition to use against you.

To conclude this section, we have a responsibility as teachers to uphold public trust in the profession and maintain high standards of conduct in line with the Teachers' Standards. Of course, we should be allowed to enjoy ourselves and socialise, but we must also accept the added level of responsibility that results from the privileged position that we hold.

These examples are not intended to worry or scare individuals, but to raise awareness of the need to act as role models both inside and outside school. We are still role models when we leave the school gates, just as police officers are expected to act accordingly once they leave their stations.

Finally, if we do something that brings our reputation or public trust in our profession into doubt, we can be sure that the information will get back to the headteacher, whether they are present or not.

Top Tip: Configure social media settings accurately. Configure your social media account settings carefully to ensure you protect yourself from any unintended embarrassment. You may want to anonymise your name on social media accounts or ensure that your accounts are private and locked down to ensure pupils can't find any information about you. Pupils are naturally inquisitive and may try to search for you. Protect yourself and others from anything you wouldn't want pupils or colleagues to see. **#TeachingTopTip**

TAKE OWNERSHIP

As a reader of this book, you're an individual who takes responsibility for their own development, so I may be preaching to the converted. Unfortunately, not every teacher is like you.

There are many teachers who never take ownership of themselves and always to try to blame others for their poor performance. These teachers are in every school, deflecting any sort of responsibility from themselves onto any other person or thing they can find. Don't be that person.

These are the teachers who constantly make excuses. They might complain the projector didn't work, the computers were down, the photocopier broke this morning, or the classroom was too hot. They'll claim 'these pupils don't want to learn' or try the rather common excuse that it was windy outside! Rather than looking inward, they can't believe that they have done anything to warrant their own problems. Luckily for me, these teachers are unlikely to be reading this book, as they will believe they are the finished article. They are not, and they will soon be found out (if they haven't been already).

Instead of blaming everything and everyone else, I encourage you firstly to look inward. Be reflective. Was my lesson planned as well as it could have been? Did I have all of my slides ready? Did I have an activity ready for pupils to begin on their arrival? Are my pupils in a set routine? Am I prepared for the lesson? Have I got the equipment I need? Did I arrive at the class before the pupils? Have I photocopied all the relevant worksheets, and do I know where everything is? Is the seating plan correct? Are the windows open before lunch to cool the classroom down on a hot summer's day? Am I meeting and greeting at the door to check uniform and behaviour on entry to my classroom? Am I calling home to reward and encourage good behaviour? These are the sort of questions you should be asking when you are teaching and more importantly after you have taught a lesson you think has gone badly.

It is much easier to blame others than to improve yourself. Don't be that person. Remember, you can't control the weather or the fact that some of your pupils haven't worn coats outside in a torrential downpour. You can't control whether they have just come from a lesson with a supply teacher where they messed around for an hour, or whether some of the pupils in your class have fallen out with each other before they arrive at your lesson. You can't control whether they have eaten breakfast or lunch.

What you can control is your classroom environment. You set the weather inside your classroom; don't let anyone else tell you otherwise!

Teachers will say that last lesson on a Friday is the worst time to teach pupils, or that because it is windy outside the pupils won't listen to you. My personal opinion is that this is nonsense. Much of it can become a self-fulfilling prophecy if we're not careful.

TAKE CRITICISM ON THE CHIN

Criticism and advice can hurt. It can be painful. But it is important that, within context, you try and listen to it. Use your own internal filter to decide whether some of the criticism needs to be discarded straight away but also be mindful to the fact that some of it may really benefit your practice. I like to think that most of the criticism teachers receive from colleagues is constructive and I certainly try and take that mindset myself.

Try to be the teacher who takes criticism head on. Take it in, reflect on it, test it out, evaluate the results, and then make your mind up. Earlier, we spoke about being humble and the need to appreciate and understand that you are not the finished article. Most colleagues give feedback because they care, and they want to see you improve. You should be more concerned if people stop giving you feedback, as this may indicate a belief that you won't listen to it anyway.

No matter what you do, treat criticism (and anything that you do in school for that matter) as a learning experience. Whatever happens, learn from it and endeavour not to repeat the same mistakes again.

I remember one teacher I worked with who just could not take any advice I gave them. The advice was offered in the spirit of helping to improve their teaching, but it wasn't welcomed. The teacher in question came across as if they knew everything and believed it could not possibly be anything to do with themselves. Don't be that individual. Your mentors and colleagues aren't obliged to give you advice; it's quite the opposite. They are giving you advice because they want you to improve your practice. Listen, take it in and try it out. You have nothing to lose. Once you have tried their feedback, and are still not convinced, your mentor or colleague will be more than happy to go back to the drawing board and think of some other strategies because they know you are listening to their improvements. Teaching is a skill that constantly needs to be refined. No one is ever the finished product.

Control the controllables

In school, there are things that you can control, and things that you can't control. One of the best ways to stay sane and to support your personal wellbeing is to concentrate on things that are within your control.

If you're anything like I was when I first started teaching, you will constantly question why things are done a certain way. You will look at systems, processes and procedures and think they could be done in different, more efficient ways. It is important to make a note of these, as some day you may wish to improve them yourself, but for now it is vital to master one thing at a time.

When you start teaching, you should use all your energy to make your lessons as good as they can be and your teaching as effective as possible. Over time, once your teaching is solid and you are confident that you have the basics sorted, you can begin to expand your sphere of influence and get involved in improving other aspects.

First, however, it is essential that your teaching is up to scratch. That's what you're paid to do, and it's the single thing that makes the biggest difference to pupil outcomes. Concentrate on that first. Once you become a strong teacher, you will find your credibility will soar and you will be able to use this to your advantage when influencing change on a larger scale.

Once you are an excellent teacher and are looking to make a greater impact, offer solutions, not problems. If you identify something that you think could be improved, try to think of a solution to fix the problem. Teachers at all levels are extremely busy, so if you present them with a solution, they are likely to be much more grateful than if they perceive you are adding more items to their To Do list. They may even offer you the chance to take the lead in solving the problem you have identified, which is a fantastic way for you to widen your sphere of influence within the school as well.

Top Tip: Concentrate on your teaching first. When you enter this wonderful profession, you may question everything that you see and want to make improvements. You should make a note of these so you can potentially make changes in the future, but first you should concentrate on becoming a strong teacher. Your credibility will soar, and colleagues will then be more likely to take your suggestions on board. Teaching is also the job you are being paid for, so you need to prioritise this at all times. **#TeachingTopTip**

INVEST IN YOURSELF

One of the best pieces of advice I can offer is to invest in yourself continually, be it physically, academically or mentally. When you first start teaching, the demands will be intense, so you will need to look after yourself and listen to what your body is telling you. If you need to sleep, sleep. If you need to exercise, exercise.

Always look for anything you can use to improve your own teaching. Once you have knowledge, no one can take it away from you and you can apply it to develop your own teaching.

TWITTER

Social media can be an incredible source of professional development as a teacher. There are many teachers who blog about their work and many subject pedagogy discussions are discussed over Twitter. I would strongly recommend setting up an account and following teachers to offer a new insight into different activities.

One caveat is that you need to ignore, silence or block any negativity. Some teachers use social media as an outlet for their frustrations and concerns, and sometimes teaching debates can get heated. Remember, stay positive and remove the negativity from your newsfeed.

Top Tip: **Sign up to Twitter**. Follow educators from your own discipline and more widely to build up a diverse knowledge of teaching techniques and pedagogy. Keep your feed positive by blocking any negativity. #TeachingTopTip

ADDITIONAL QUALIFICATIONS

There are some nationally recognised qualifications, and your school is likely to support some teachers on these courses each year. Experience may play some part in being chosen, but it is not the only attribute that school leaders will consider when deciding who they will fund on a course.

Being proactive about looking for courses is one way of ensuring your name is at the front of the list for acceptance onto a course. There are myriad courses out there that will suit individuals, but you cannot expect anyone other than yourself to find these for you. Why would your headteacher know you had a keen interest in improving your teaching to EAL pupils (pupils with English as an additional language) unless they have seen you demonstrating it? Search for courses online, ask colleagues if they have attended any useful courses, and ask questions on Twitter.

I would always encourage new teachers to take up opportunities to grow and develop. Listen to others who have different opinions to yourself. Attend conferences. Some take place on Saturdays, but the energy they give you to take back to your job is well worth it. You feel energised spending time with like-minded teachers. This is not for everyone, I get that.

But if you can spare the occasional Saturday for a conference like ResearchED, you will not be disappointed.

Not only are there conferences and free CPD on the internet, but there is a whole wealth of teaching and learning literature being written at the moment which offers a large range of opportunities to grow as a teacher and learn new skills to try in the classroom.

TeachMeets

Although most development is likely to cost the school a quantity of money, there are often free local events that you can attend to develop yourself. TeachMeets are gatherings of local teachers to discuss certain aspects of teaching or pedagogy. The sessions are attended by like-minded teachers aiming to develop their own practice. As these are often voluntary meetings which take place after school, they are a great way to share knowledge and network with like-minded individuals.

These events are often publicised online, through social media and by word-of-mouth, so keep a look-out; they are well worth attending.

Lead without a title

Once you have become more accomplished as a teacher, you may be looking for more opportunities to grow, lead and develop others. Without making an effort to look, you will spot areas or processes in your school that you think could be improved or developed. You may have recently attended a course or a conference and realise that some of the elements could be usefully incorporated within your department or more widely within the school.

Although you may have identified key areas where you perceive you can add value, you might not believe you can enact change without a leadership role or additional responsibilities. Many teachers think titles are important.

This is not the case; not holding a specific title or a responsibility does not prevent you from implementing change. School leaders will be delighted that you are offering support. Remember, though, that the best way to enact change within a school is to offer solutions, not potential or current problems.

The notion of titles within schools intrigues me. Think about this. If you removed every title from every member of staff in a school, who would the staff or pupils say is the head-teacher, the deputy, the behaviour manager, the admin manager and so on? I think in some schools, the individuals that pupils select wouldn't necessarily match the position they have been given. Some will be performing better than their job description, whilst others will fall short.

Just because you haven't got a Second in Department or a Head of Department role, it doesn't mean you are not capable of change. If you have the capacity to solve a problem, step up to the plate and own it.

But a word of caution is needed: remember, your teaching needs to be excellent before you enact change. Then you will have built up your credibility and your line managers and colleagues won't think you are trying to do too much too soon.

DEALING WITH PARENTS

Working with parents can be a powerful way of leveraging the impact you have as a teacher within the classroom. If you can get parents on board with your teaching strategies and behaviour management and can develop a good rapport with them, they will save you an awful lot of time in the long run.

Earlier, we discussed the power of ringing home as early as possible in the school year and building a positive relationship with parents. It is much easier to ask parents to support you when disciplining their child if you have called them previously and been positive. Parents will appreciate that you are a fair teacher who will praise and apply sanctions when appropriate.

It is also worth noting that parents may have also had a problematic time at school themselves. They may still harbour thoughts and grievances about their own time at school, which will be through no fault of your own. Working with parents in a positive way can reap significant dividends over time and you should always look to maximise their influence. It will help you to ensure your pupils do as well as they can, both behaviourally and academically.

PARENTS' EVENINGS

Nowadays, I find parents' evenings hugely beneficial, as I know parents can be such an effective lever to use when motivating, supporting and challenging my pupils to improve. However, at the start of my teaching career, I had no idea what I was doing. At my first parents' evening, I was clueless about what to say or do. I was supposed to talk about every child in five minutes for three hours straight, with limited breaks.

Ok, so what do I now do to prepare?

Ultimately, what do you think parents want to know? All they're interested in is whether their child is doing well or not. If they're doing well, that's fantastic; they can encourage their child to keep doing what they're doing and look for marginal gains to improve even further. If they're performing badly, what can they do to help and improve their child's education? I think that's what it boils down to.

If you stick to the basics, you can't go wrong and your first parents' evening shouldn't be anything to worry about.

Everyone has had a difficult child in their class and has been concerned about what to say to their parents. However, I have always thought that parents want to hear the honest truth, even if it is hard to take. Be frank and honest, but at least try to highlight something that their child has done well. You want the meeting to be agreeable, but you also need to tell parents or carers if their child needs to improve in certain areas.

If you are struggling to decide how to talk to each parent and structure your response, a common approach is for negative comments to be sandwiched between two positive statements. This provides a more rigorous structure and the balance it provides does seem like a suitable way of giving feedback. For some, this will appear too rigid and they will find a more natural style.

As parents' evenings are normally very busy, it is vital that you keep to time as much as possible. Some parents will be running late so it may be possible to squeeze in a parent earlier than their allocated slot. You should try your best to keep speaking to parents. In my experience, it is not always possible to keep to the order on your timetable sheet. If a parent is overrunning somewhere else, I would first see other parents who are waiting to see you, to ensure you don't run further behind.

Top Tip: If you are trying to close your appointment and you sense that the parents want to keep talking, one tip is to stand up once their session is nearing the end. This acts as a signal, making it easier for you to dismiss parents.

If they persist in talking, you can say that you have lots of parents to see (in the nicest possible way of course) and that if they want to continue the conversation you are happy to arrange a separate meeting another time or ring them. #**TeachingTopTip**

At parents' evenings, be careful that you don't promise too much. Parents will want to know if you can do x, y, z for their child and if you're not careful, you will effectively be writing a long To Do list for yourself for the following day. Where necessary, you can offer to print an extra sheet or provide some extra support here and there, but be mindful that if you do that for every parent, you will create a lot of extra tasks on top of your own day-to-day workload. You may also let parents down if you can't meet a commitment you agreed to at the parents' evening.

Another piece of good practice is to print off the class marksheet from your school's data provider or from records you have made. It is useful to have that in front of you when you are having a parents' evening appointment; you can quickly find each pupil and have all the data you need to hand.

Some parents like to see their child's books, so it could be worth having the class pile next to you if you wish, but I don't think it is essential. You don't have much time to speak to parents, so spending time finding their book is not always as beneficial as talking and providing feedback to individual parents.

Don't be disheartened if some parents don't seem to care. I will never forget one of my first ever parents' evenings. I was telling some parents about their child's wonderful work in maths, saying that she was capable of doing so well at maths and how brilliant the work in her book was. Her father interrupted, 'Mate, I'm not being funny, but when will she ever need to learn this? The only maths I use is on a darts board.'

At the time, I was demoralised; I seriously questioned what I was doing. Just remember, we've all had experiences like that, and as teachers we all have stories to tell, no matter how long we've been in the profession.

Parents' evenings can be tremendously impactful in leveraging the work and attitude of their children within your classroom. Even though it may be more difficult to deliver, make sure parents hear the messages that they need to hear, not simply pleasantries that don't push on their child's learning.

EXTRA-CURRICULAR ACTIVITIES

Whether you are in a sports team, music group or any form of extra-curricular activity, I urge you to keep it up during your teaching career. Yes, your first year will be busy and stressful at times, but you need to ensure you maintain your own hobbies and manage your time effectively.

I know too many teachers who have stopped their own leisure activities to devote more time to teaching. The danger is that your job becomes all-consuming and you start to lose enthusiasm for the profession because it stops you from doing what you enjoy.

· · ·

RUNNING AN EXTRA-CURRICULAR ACTIVITY

Running an extra-curricular activity at school is a great way of using some of your expertise and developing pupils in your specialist area. It is also an excellent way to build your presence around the school, get to know more pupils that you might not teach, and contribute more widely to the school environment in which you work.

I am a keen musician and sportsman, and I refereed football matches for over ten years, so I could offer the school quite a lot in extra-curricular activities. However, it is important not to attempt to be a superstar when you first enter a school. It is so easy to commit to starting a club, offering your services here, there and everywhere, but it is much harder to stop. If you are new to the profession, don't offer your extra-curricular services too soon. You may find that your time is stretched, and it puts extra pressure on you in the long term.

It is also important to be aware of the honeymoon period. You may start teaching and after a couple of weeks think you are smashing it and are ready to start a club. It is most likely you are in the honeymoon period. Pupils are still trying to work you out, so they aren't showing their true colours. You are still full of adrenaline at starting the job and this is not the best time to make any decisions.

I would wait until after the first whole term before making any decisions on supporting or starting any extra-curricular activities. This will still give you plenty of time to help out, but it will provide you with the necessary grounding in your teaching before you spread yourself too thinly to start with.

Top Tip: Don't commit too early. You may be keen to help with extra-curricular activities. I would recommend you wait until at least the end of one whole term before jumping in to start a club. It is much easier to say you'll help out than end up pulling out after a few weeks.

When you first start at the school, try not to publish your skills and hidden qualities to everyone, because you will be inundated with people trying to get you to help. This may be well-intentioned but deep down, the teachers may just be trying to pass off their club to a keen NQT who can relieve them of some of their workload. Be careful! **#TeachingTopTip**

CAREER ADVICE NO ONE EVER TELLS YOU ABOUT

APPLYING FOR JOBS

The teaching profession is currently facing a severe recruitment and retention crisis. Yet the impact of this varies regionally and in different subjects. For example, maths teachers in most parts of the country have a much greater choice and can almost pick the school they want to work in. They are in such short supply that headteachers are becoming frantic in their attempt to recruit them. In other subjects where supply outstrips demand, it may be more difficult to find employment, but you should not be disheartened.

If you do find yourself in a situation where you are desperately wanted and you sense that there is great demand for your services, you can use this to your advantage, as I will explain in more depth later on.

WHEN TO APPLY?

Due to the shortage of teachers, job adverts can appear all

year around. Certain websites are used primarily for advertising teacher positions: eTeach and TES. The government offers a teacher vacancy service although, at the time of writing, it is in its infancy. On these sites, you can create job alerts so that you receive an e-mail every time a new job fitting your criteria arises. This is a great way to hunt for jobs passively.

Although teacher recruitment does happen throughout the year, there are times where jobs are more likely to come up. I have always found the period between Christmas and Easter and the weeks leading up to the May half term to be the busiest.

DON'T RUSH BUT DON'T DELAY

Although during your training year you will be understandably anxious about finding a teaching job for September, you shouldn't rush in and apply for any old job. Do the research on your chosen school and consider whether it would be a good fit for you.

It is common practice to visit the school beforehand if you can, to get a feel for it before you apply. Although a visit is not always possible, it certainly helps you to be better informed.

Trainee teachers will all be in the same position hunting for jobs; as Easter approaches, you therefore don't want to be in a situation where you haven't applied for any jobs. That will make you more vulnerable, as a lot of positions will have already been filled by then.

For a September start, teachers have to hand in their resignation at their current school by 31st May, giving two months' notice (excluding the Summer holiday). Therefore, if you are in the unique position of not having a current employer and are still in your training year, there may still be further opportunities after this date to find a teaching job, although you certainly shouldn't bank on it.

Overall, I would recommend you start looking and applying for jobs from January to maximise the chances of securing a job in a school that you would love to work in. As time goes by, job opportunities may fall, and you may find yourself with a reduced selection of jobs to apply for.

THE INTERVIEW PROCESS

Teaching is slightly unusual in its approach to recruitment compared to the private sector, in that a decision on who to appoint is taken on the day itself. You should expect to receive a phone call in the early evening after your interview, either offering you a job or regretfully turning you down.

THE DAY ITSELF

After shortlisting, you will receive an invitation to interview. You should understand that you are under scrutiny from the minute you receive this invitation; those leading the recruitment may make judgements about you from your response to the e-mail. It is also becoming increasingly common for employers to look at your online presence. Remember, everyone has an online profile and if you have something that you would be embarrassed about if it were brought up at interview, it is advisable to take it down. This links to my earlier recommendation to configure your privacy settings correctly to avoid unintended embarrassment.

Not only will you have been evaluated before you arrive at your interview, but anything you do on the day may be mentioned to the panel. It is not just the formal elements that will be assessed. How you communicate with the receptionist, cleaners, any other staff and pupils around the site will all be noted and could be passed on.

Some candidates shoot themselves in the foot by being rude to receptionists and other staff they encounter informally on their interview day, relaxing their guard as they do not think it is part of the interview process. Getting into lively debates with prospective colleagues is not the wisest choice to make either. In a school, everyone is part of the same team, and if a teacher can't manage the basics of presenting themselves well at interview, there isn't much hope moving forward.

Arrival

You will have been given a time to arrive on your interview day. Be on time, but not too early. I recommend that you plan your route in advance. Get to the school much earlier than necessary, then park in an adjacent road. You may think that arriving 30 minutes before your arrival time shows you are keen enough to put in extra effort, but receptionists are busy. If you arrive too early, they may feel under pressure to accommodate you in that time. I'd wait in the car and then arrive no more than 10 minutes before your appointment time. This still gives you enough time to settle before the interview day starts.

Remember the basics of being respectful and courteous to *everyone* you meet. You never know who you are speaking to or what connections they may have. Make eye contact, give a firm handshake and be confident. Believe in yourself. You belong there and they have shortlisted you, so be prepared to go and boss the day!

Don't stand out for the wrong reasons. I was once running an interview panel and the headteacher's secretary offered the candidates a drink at the beginning of the day. One of the candidates asked if it was possible to have a fruit tea and said that he had brought a tea bag of his own. Now, I may be alone here, but this struck me as a very bizarre request for someone new to a school and attending an interview. Just remember that people will be making judgements the whole time, intentionally or subconsciously. You only get one chance to make a good first impression!

BRIEFING

The day will usually start with the headteacher or another member of the Senior Leadership Team (SLT) welcoming candidates to the school, providing a bit of background and giving you an itinerary. This is your chance to make a good first impression on the staff leading the interviews, so it is important to put your best foot forward.

Interview days tend to consist of a variety of activities that candidates will do on a rotational basis. They may include teaching a lesson, facing a pupil panel, and a tour of the school, before finishing with an interview panel. You could be given a data task, although this tends to be mainly for leadership roles. A data task could involve giving you a class set of data and asking you to identify three elements from it that stand out. It may be that boys are outperforming girls, pupils with special educational needs or disabilities (SEND) are making significantly lower progress than their peers, or that higher attaining pupils aren't making as much progress as others.

TOUR OF THE SCHOOL

The day may begin with an informal tour led by pupils.

This provides an opportunity to get a feel for the school by observing lessons, watching behaviour and asking pupils any questions you may have. The tour can be done singly, in pairs or as a small group, depending on the number of candidates. Pupils may ask if there are any areas you'd like to look at, so consider in advance if there are any areas you are particularly keen to see.

Although this tour is informal, pupils may be asked for their views on the candidates later, so be polite and respectful. Remember, you cannot let your guard down at any point during the interview day. A slip of the tongue or a rogue comment may ruin all of the solid work you have done or are going to do later in the day.

Pupil panel

You may also be asked to take part in a pupil panel. The common convention is for candidates to attend individual sessions, with about three pupils asking and recording answers to their questions. You will often see a teacher or secretary making notes. The panel may meet several candidates together; however, this is less common.

Pupils may have come up with the questions themselves, so be ready for some 'random' questions. The aim of this task is to see how you relate to pupils and what they think of you. While the overall judgement on whether or not to offer you a job is not likely to be based solely on the pupil panel, it does form a part of the triangulation approach schools will use to assess your capabilities.

It is worth asking and learning the pupils' names, showing an interest in them and finding out what they like about the school, then trying to answer the questions as honestly as you can. Remember that you are at an interview and your answers are likely to be recorded. You may tend to be more honest to pupils than you would be in a formal interview, but remember that everything you say will still be noted and passed on.

It can be very hard to predict what questions a pupil panel will ask, but the best advice is to be yourself. If you enjoy working with children, can build a rapport with pupils and have a few interests, you should be fine.

Some questions that pupils may ask are:

- What's your favourite film/sweet/drink and why?
- Why are you a teacher?
- What would you do if someone in the class was misbehaving?
- What is the proudest moment of your teaching career?
- Tell us a joke.

Although the last one is not strictly a question, it does frequently come up in pupil panels; I think some pupils must think teachers are somehow wannabe stand-up comedians. Putting you on the spot like that in a pressured environment is difficult, so it could be worth learning a couple of one-liners appropriate for pupil ears, just in case.

INTERVIEW LESSON

Arguably one of the most important parts of the day, your interview lesson is the chance for you to show the skill you are being employed for: your teaching. You might have been asked to bring a printed lesson plan for the individuals observing your lesson. It is also good practice to print your slides in advance so you can give these to the observers too.

The preparation for your interview lesson should start as

soon as you receive the topic. You are likely to receive an e-mail containing the lesson topic, prior attainment level of pupils and basic information about the class when you are invited to interview. You may get an instruction such as 'Teach adding fractions with different denominators to a low attaining Year 7 group. They are set 5 of 6. Your lesson should be 25 minutes long.' You are unlikely to get much more information, but you have a topic and a starting point.

Once you receive this information, start preparing the lesson as you would normally teach it. Do not assume the school will have the same resources as your own. They may have different textbooks, no textbooks, no mini whiteboards, and no rulers. Never assume anything.

The key for interview lessons is to take *everything* you need with you. Be prepared. For a maths interview, I would take a ream of squared paper, a box of calculators, spare pens, whiteboard pens, rulers, and any other equipment I think may be necessary for my interview lesson. Preparation is key.

I would also prepare my lesson in PowerPoint (even though I don't normally use PowerPoint for my lessons) as it is a universal program that every school will have. I would save my slides on a memory stick and a cloud-based system as well as e-mailing them to myself, to ensure that they are definitely available when I reach my interview classroom.

It is sensible to prepare a back-up plan in case the technology breaks down or doesn't work in your interview lesson. What are you going to do then? This is unlikely to happen, but if you have prepared well, you should be able to deliver the lesson you had planned without being anxious about its delivery.

If you do forget the equipment you need, there may be an opportunity to obtain it once you arrive at the school, but remember everyone in school is busy and you do not want to give them extra tasks to do if you can avoid it.

Interview lessons can pose problems for teachers at all stages of their career. They involve unfamiliar computers and new pupils in a strange environment and are almost always only about 20-25 minutes long, which is never enough time to complete what you had planned. Don't worry; it happens to everyone and this will be taken into account.

Observers will be looking for some of the following: the clarity of your explanations, how well you relate to pupils, whether you learn pupils' names and can remind pupils who are drifting off task to regain their focus, whether you are able to issue praise, are relatable and personable with pupils, and have charisma or personality.

As a teacher at interview, you are never going to be able to pitch your lesson at exactly the right level, as you don't know much about the pupils in your class. You won't know all their names because you have never met them before. However, observers do get a sense of whether someone has 'presence' in a classroom and could control a class on their own.

At the end of the interview lesson, you may be asked to step outside whilst the people who watched your lesson speak to the class to seek their feedback. This is normal and shouldn't alarm you. You will then be escorted back to the staff room or your base for the day. It is understandable that you might not have taught the lesson as well as you had hoped, or that you missed out a few elements, but don't beat yourself up about it.

There is likely to be an opportunity to discuss the lesson with your observer/s later in the day; one of the skills they are looking for is your ability to be reflective. If you draw out the same positive and negative aspects of your lesson as they've seen, it will make a favourable impression; you will be regarded as someone who knows the areas they need to improve and develop, in addition to the elements that are strong. This is a key trait of excellent teachers.

Top Tip: Take everything you need for your interview lesson. Never assume that the school where you are being interviewed will have the same equipment as your own school. Take lined paper, pens, pencils, rulers, compasses etc. Make sure your lesson is on a memory stick or cloud-based storage and that you've e-mailed it to yourself, but also have a back-up in case the technology fails. Be prepared. #TeachingTopTip

---

INTERVIEW

Your day is likely to culminate in an interview with members of the Senior Leadership Team and usually the Head of Department. Although these are the people that will ultimately make the decision about whether or not to appoint you, they are still human beings. They are just like you, only perhaps a few years further along their teaching journey. You shouldn't fear them. Have respect for yourself, hold yourself in high regard and perform to the best of your ability. The interview panel want you to succeed and are giving you an opportunity to sell yourself.

It's important to be aware that the panel asks the same questions for each candidate in the job. This rule ensures fairness in the recruitment process. Follow-up questions will obviously differ, but the original questions must be the same for all candidates.

A helpful way to answer questions is through the STAR approach which you may or may not be familiar with: Situation, Task, Action, Result. Firstly, you explain the situation and environment that your example sits within. You then identify the specific task that you had to complete, say how you did it and finish by explaining its impact. This helps give a structure to your answers and enables you to be concise.

The panel members are likely to ask each question in turn, but you should make eye contact and communicate with all of them when answering. It's normal for them to take notes as you give your responses, because they need to score them against pre-agreed criteria. They may just be copying down what you are saying in order to make comparisons with the other candidates later on, so don't worry if they are writing while you speak, although admittedly it can be unnerving.

The questions may vary, depending on your subject or whether any leadership responsibility is attached to the job. As a general guide, the following could arise:

- Why are you a teacher?
- Talk to me about your lesson. What went well and what could be improved?
- Where does your lesson fit within the sequence of lessons?
- Why do you want to teach at School X?
- A safeguarding question e.g. 'A pupil stays behind at break time and asks to speak to you. They disclose something about what happened at home over the weekend. What do you do?'
- What would be the good features of a subject lesson?

- How would you react if a pupil misbehaved in your lesson?
- What would you do if you noticed a pupil falling behind?
- How would you monitor pupil progress over time?
- Do you have any questions for us?
- Do you have any professional development needs?*
- If offered the job today, would you accept?**

You may be tempted to script responses to all of these questions above. This may help you get your thoughts down on paper, but trying to remember them is not an effective use of time, and you may be asked different questions.

Prepare some points you think are important to mention and try to include them in your responses, but only if they are relevant. Don't leave the interview regretting that you didn't make those impressive points you had identified beforehand.

Interviewers may ask if you want to mention anything else that you haven't had the opportunity to tell them. This allows you another chance to make the key points you thought of beforehand.

The interview can also be the best time to discuss pay and salary, but I will cover this topic in the next chapter.

*Professional development needs: this question is not always asked, but it is a great opportunity to share your ambitions with the panel and make them aware of your intended trajectory and how you wish to develop your skills within the profession.

If you have a course in mind that you would like to go on, or you are interested in visiting other schools to see how they teach the subject, now is the time to raise it. Perhaps you aspire to have some subject leadership in the future and would relish the opportunity for development relevant to that. It's useful if you have a few ideas like this ready for your interview. The school leaders, if they're worth their salt, will want to develop their staff; they may have a policy of internal promotions as part of their recruitment and retention strategy.

** The knowledge of whether you would accept the job if it was offered to you is an extremely important question, so let's explore it further.

ACCEPTING OR REJECTING A JOB OFFER

Recruiting teachers is a costly exercise. For a school, it includes the direct cost of advertising plus leaders' time, so the total can run into thousands of pounds per vacancy. Schools don't have the money to recruit, recruit, recruit. Additionally, if the recruitment process takes place close to the final deadline for achieving a September start (31st May), schools may also not have time to appoint anyone else if they don't recruit on that day.

After the 31st May deadline has passed, schools will only be able to recruit teachers without existing teaching jobs for a September start: those who are finishing their training years or are returning to teach from a different career.

Therefore, if a school offers you a job, they are expecting you to accept. If you decide it's not the job for you after the headteacher has made you an offer on the phone, it is considered bad form and it won't go down well, as schools may have to complete the recruitment process again at considerable cost.

However, pulling out of a job whilst you're at the school is nothing to worry about. Leaders at the school are not just interviewing you; you are interviewing the school and if it is not the right fit, it is fine to walk out.

If you decide it doesn't feel right, be cordial and respectful, and explain your decision, preferably to the headteacher themselves or another appropriate person. If you say that you have enjoyed the experience but on reflection it is not the right school for you, it may be upsetting for them, but they will appreciate your honesty. It is far better for both parties that the individual they appoint is not only suitable but also wants to be in the post.

An interview is a two-way process

When the panel members ask you if you have any questions, it is your opportunity to make honest enquiries about the school. As a new teacher, it may be important to find out how the leaders approach behaviour management and what support they offer to staff.

Questions that will give you a better understanding of the school could include: Why is this vacancy open? What behaviour support is there within the school? What are the strengths/development areas that the school has? What opportunities are there for professional development?

As already noted, this also provides an opportunity to discuss contractual obligations such as pay, which will be discussed in the next chapter.

Receiving the phone call

Once the interview is over, you will leave and wait at home for a phone call. After a few hours (some schools are quicker than others), you will receive a phone call from the head-teacher or the department head, either offering you the job or saying you weren't successful on this occasion.

. . .

ACCEPTING THE OFFER

If you are offered the job, remain professional and thank them. You will receive a letter of employment shortly afterwards. Be aware that the letter is not a contract at this stage; that will come a short while later. They will invite you to complete the paperwork for your safeguarding checks (DBS in the UK) and will ask you to bring in your original documents for their own checks.

Remember that you are still employed by your current employer until the first day at your new school. It would be foolish to do something inappropriate or unprofessional between the receipt of a job offer and the day you start your new job. This interim phase may occur over a holiday period, but you should still remember who your current employer is. If training, your job will be dependent on successful completion of your training year which your current school will ultimately be in charge of signing off.

INFORMING YOUR OWN SCHOOL

Upon returning to your own school after the interview, your headteacher is likely to ask how you did. They are doing this for two main reasons. Firstly, and I hope most importantly, they are genuinely interested in your career and want to know if you got the job. Secondly, if you are an existing member of staff rather than a trainee teacher, they are working out whether they need to start the recruitment process for your replacement.

This is generally not a problem for trainee teachers looking for their first post, as they are not actually employed by the school. For existing members of staff, it can be a more pressing issue.

Headteachers, particularly those within multi-academy

trusts, are often prevented from advertising for a post until the teacher who is leaving formally resigns. As a result, head-teachers will be eager to replace you if you are an existing member of staff and may try and pressurise you to send your resignation letter in before you receive a contract from your new employer. I would try and resist their request where possible. It is recommended that a teacher should not resign until they have received and signed their contract. This is a sensible move, to protect themselves.

In this situation, the headteacher is asking you to bear the risk that you won't receive the contract. If your job offer falls through, you will be without a job, and the school won't be obliged to take you back. I must emphasise that this is a rare event.

If you receive a letter of employment but for some reason you don't receive a contract, seek union guidance; even so, I recommend you protect yourself by only handing in your resignation letter once you have signed your new contract. It is an extra layer of protection, covering yourself in case anything untoward happens. Your current headteacher will have to wait or take the risk themselves.

Just be cautious; without being rude, let your headteacher know you will submit your resignation letter as soon as you receive a contract confirming your appointment.

The only exception is where you are employed by a school already and are approaching the final deadline for a September start (31st May). In this case, you may have to submit your resignation letter before you receive a contract, as I will explain later. Don't worry if you find yourself in this situation; it happens all the time. Wherever possible though, I'd wait until you receive your contract, to cover yourself.

. . .

DEALING WITH REJECTION

Rejection can hurt in any event or walk of life. If you are rejected from a job, take it on the chin and move on. You will never know exactly what the panel were looking for and you will have learnt a great deal from the experience.

Ensure that you either get feedback over the phone or arrange a time to discuss the outcome with the headteacher. Any reasonable school leader will be happy to do this. Take their feedback on board and listen. You may disagree with some of the advice, and that's fine. Other aspects, however, may be very useful and you can develop them ready for your next interview.

LEAVING YOUR JOB

When the time comes to leave your job, you should be aware that you are required to give two months' notice before you leave. The reason is that it allows the school time to recruit a replacement.

Most people leave their jobs at the end of the academic year, so they can make a fresh start at the new school. The six-week holiday in between offers most people a chance to gear up for the new job.

Having said that, teachers do leave jobs within the year. The most common times for this are at the close of each big term (Christmas or Easter). The table below shows the resignation dates required to start a post on each start date. The earlier resignation date to start a new job in September is due to the fact that recruitment won't happen over the six-week summer holiday.

Resignation date	Start date
31st October	1st January
28th February	1st May
31st May	1st September

A WORD OF CAUTION

If you are resigning with effect from the end of the academic year, be aware of the timing difficulties it presents for the headteacher of your current school. Consider their recruitment process for your replacement; it needs to be completed by 31st May, the deadline for you to hand in your notice. Little wonder that headteachers across the country are on tenterhooks for several months before this date, because they are not 100% sure which of their staff will be returning in September.

As long as you have received your contract, hand your resignation letter in as soon as possible. Your current headteacher will appreciate it, because they can get their recruitment started earlier.

As mentioned earlier, if you are successful at an interview close to the deadline of 31st May and are currently employed by the school, you may have to resign without receiving your full contract. Otherwise, you won't be able to leave and take up your new post by the start of the new school year. This is not something to worry about. It is advisable to wait for your contract if possible, as it gives you that added layer of protection, but you shouldn't worry if you are appointed close to the 31st May deadline and won't be able to receive the contract before then.

Remember that because your salary is spread across the

whole year, you are paid during the holidays. In your resignation letter you must therefore state that your last date of employment will be 31st August, so that you continue to be paid until that day. Remember, you are still employed by your current school until that date, so you should continue to act professionally and be a model employee.

LEAVING DURING THE YEAR

Although you are permitted to leave during the year, it causes disruption to pupils' learning because it is harder for schools to recruit your replacement. You may experience an atmosphere if you are in this situation, especially if you teach pupils completing exams that year; it can have a significant effect on them.

This is not intended to guilt-trip people into staying until the end of the year. Life doesn't work like that, and opportunities don't always arise as planned, but it is worth noting.

RESIGNATION LETTER AND RESIGNATION SPEECHES

Always be courteous when you are saying your farewells. Don't say something you'll later regret. Education is a small world, and everyone talks to each other. Stay out of trouble and you'll be fine. You will probably need your previous headteacher to provide a reference for your future jobs too.

I have listened to some horrifying resignation speeches that have insulted school leaders in various ways. Nothing is gained from this and it reflects badly on the individual concerned, rather than those they are trying to paint in a bad light.

In your resignation letter, I suggest you simply thank the school for its commitment and cover the technicalities of when your last day of employment will be. Let me repeat my reminder that if you are starting a job on 1st September, be sure to say your last date of employment is 31st August so you continue to be paid over the Summer, even though you may finish teaching pupils at the school in July.

CAREER PROGRESSION

When you have found your feet and feel more comfortable teaching pupils, you may start to think you'd like to progress and widen your sphere of influence. This is not always the case, and individuals without the desire to become a school leader have an essential part to play within education; they should not be pushed into a pathway they do not wish to explore.

The important thing to note is that no one cares about your career as much as you do. Within teaching, there is sometimes a perception that class teachers without additional teaching and learning responsibilities (TLRs) are not as driven or determined as individuals seeking to climb the leadership ladder. This is not the case. I regularly meet teachers who have devoted their entire careers to teaching their subjects to a high standard. They have no ambition to take on leadership responsibilities, but they are more than content teaching their own subject and sharing that passion with other pupils. Their contribution is valuable; as a profession, we must never forget this.

If you do wish to progress to leadership, it is important to take care of yourself. As I've said, you are the best person to look after your career. You will know your aims, ambitions, and desired trajectory better than anyone else. Teaching is by and large a meritocratic profession. I have found that school leaders do look at your experience and impact within your current role before taking decisions on promotion, but they award positions on merit.

It is also worth mentioning that there are two main routes into whole school leadership: the subject leader route, and the pastoral route. The subject leader route would usually involve focusing on your subject, becoming second in charge of a department, before becoming the Head of Department and then commonly reaching the Senior Leadership Team as an Assistant Head involved with teaching and learning. The pastoral route may involve becoming a Head of Year, Head of House or helping support vulnerable or disadvantaged pupils or those with special educational needs, before moving into a pastoral position on the SLT.

Schools need diverse leaders, so there are many avenues you can explore to develop your own career in teaching.

For those looking to progress to the next level of leadership or responsibility within the profession, I would speak firstly to the post holders of your intended role within your current school to find out more about the role and what it entails. I would also recommend looking at job recruitment sites and downloading job descriptions and person specifications for the role.

The important point here is that when applying for a job, you will be judged against the essential criteria specified on person specifications. If you don't meet these, you are unlikely to be shortlisted for an interview. There will also be a column for desirable qualities; where there is strong competition for the job, you will be assessed against many of these as well.

By looking at these specifications, you can measure yourself against the essential and desirable criteria in each job advert. Then, you can cross out the qualifications or criteria that you meet and highlight the ones you don't currently have in your armoury. You will know that these are the elements you need to improve in order to make the next step in your leadership journey.

Some of these items may not fit neatly into your current role. You may need line management experience, but your current role may not allow for it, or else you are required to understand quality assurance procedures or have experience of running extra-curricular clubs.

Where elements of the criteria could be applied to your current role, there is nothing stopping you from developing the skills and knowledge straight away. Reading books, attending conferences or listening to educational podcasts are easy ways for you to develop your professional knowledge and put yourself ahead of others looking for job opportunities.

Where elements are harder to incorporate in your current role, you must be proactive and ask your line manager or headteacher for opportunities to build your career portfolio. They are not obliged to come offering the opportunity; you are in charge of your career. Yes, you might need to be brave to ask for these, but from my experience senior leaders will be more than happy to help by delegating responsibilities. The reasons for this are twofold: first, most school leaders like empowering others and seeing colleagues developing and investing in themselves, and second, it will mean they are offloading part of their workload onto you.

I can imagine you asking if you'll be paid for this added responsibility. The short answer is likely to be no. School budgets are tight and there is no magic money tree, so many of these extra responsibilities are likely to be unpaid. However, you must think of the long-term gain. If you are looking for a step-up, you will need to demonstrate that you have been proactive and gained the necessary experience beforehand.

Top Tip: Download job descriptions and person specifications for the job above your current role. Go through all the essential and desirable criteria. Make a note of the elements that you don't yet possess and then be proactive about filling in these gaps. #TeachingTopTip

INTERVIEW PRACTICE

In order to progress up the leadership ladder, you will need to go through a rigorous recruitment procedure. If you have not recently experienced a formal interview for a leadership post, it is natural to be apprehensive about what this may entail.

Use your network; ask people you trust who have done or currently do the job you are applying for to give you advice and share the type of questions they faced in interviews for that role. This preparation will stand you in good stead when you do apply and get shortlisted for interview.

Another valuable piece of advice is to try to obtain a few higher-level interviews before you're ready for the next post. Why? You might not be successful, as you may still be inexperienced for the role, but it will be excellent preparation for the round of interviews when you do want the job. You will become more comfortable with the process for that role, and you have nothing to lose if you don't receive an offer. As previously mentioned, if you use everything you ever do as a learning experience, you cannot go wrong. Learn, correct and improve.

Top Tip: Ask colleagues for information. When applying for a promoted post, ask colleagues you trust who have done or currently do the job you're applying for to give you advice and provide examples of interview questions. They will have a wealth of knowledge they'll be happy to share. **#TeachingTopTip**

PAY

The teaching profession is facing a recruitment and retention crisis. Demand is outstripping supply, which strengthens a teacher's hand and weakens a school's position in relation to pay. Government bursaries are being given out left, right and centre. Schools are providing 'golden handshakes' in certain areas and for some jobs, because they can't recruit enough teachers for specific subjects.

As a maths teacher and team leader, I can say that it is a rare occurrence for everyone in the department (or even the majority) to have studied the subject at university. There is such a shortage in many parts of the country. If you are a maths teacher, you are absolute gold dust and you will find headteachers clambering over each other to try to sign you up. You have extraordinary power.

If you are a teacher in a subject which is a bit more heavily supplied, like P.E., you may find your hand is weakened because there are more people applying for your job and demand matches supply. In some locations, supply outweighs the demand for jobs, so negotiation of pay is very challenging.

When you take a job, you are engaging in a contract between yourself and the school; no individual should go into a job application thinking it is a one-way process. We have already discussed this in the previous chapter, but it's worth remembering that an interview can involve negotiation of your pay. Headteachers won't deliberately raise this possibility, because budgets are so tight that they are not in a position to give teachers higher starting salaries without a strong reason. Training providers won't tell their trainee teachers this, because they either don't know how to advise on it or think it won't reflect well on them if all of their trainee teachers ask future employers for a higher starting salary.

Nevertheless, you are absolutely entitled to try negotiating your pay. It shows the interview panel you know your value, and it suggests you have that little bit extra about you. Let's discuss the pay structure in a little more depth before we talk specifically about negotiation.

THE PAY SCALES

Teacher pay is set out in the School Teachers' Pay and Conditions Document (STPCD). It is published annually after the Secretary of State has made recommendations on matters such as recruitment and retention, the cost of living and affordability within school budgets. There are two teaching scales which local authority maintained schools are obliged to use: the main pay scale (M1-6) and the Upper Pay Scale (UPS1-3). Academy trusts (single and multi) have autonomy and can decide to either adopt the scales or use their own.

Within the main pay scale, there are six points and they are broadly evenly spaced, with the current gap (differential) from the previous step ranging from £1,925 (M1 to M2, +7.9%) to £2,961 (M5 to M6, +9.0%). However, at the time of writing, the government is introducing a policy of increasing the starting salaries for newly qualified teachers to £30,000 by 2022 and giving bigger pay awards to early career teachers. This will squeeze the differentials between the higher points on the main scale.

In the past, the convention has been for teachers to move up one point automatically each year. However, there is now a system of performance related pay. This means that you will have annual targets and upon successful completion of these, you will be recommended for pay progression. It is important to gather evidence of your progress throughout the year, so that the headteacher can recommend you to the governing body for a pay increase. Without evidence, some governing bodies will reject the application. On the Main Pay Scale, you can usually increase one point each year although this can be negotiated as we will discuss shortly.

Once a teacher has reached M6, their salary is capped. The only way to go beyond M6 is through an application to move to the Upper Pay Scale, which has three rungs. It usually takes two years to progress up one rung on the Upper Pay Scale, as opposed to the Main Scale where it's one per year. With the current budget shortfalls, some schools could be reluctant to put teachers onto the Upper Pay Scale ('go through the threshold') because the money could be spent on other resources. This means the criteria are often more stringent.

Regardless of your current pay point, anyone can apply to move onto the Upper Pay Scale (but only once per year) in line with their school's policy. However, they will need to prove that they are 'highly competent' and that their impact is 'substantial and sustained' which will be defined in the school's pay policy. Schools often consider the last phrase, substantial and sustained, to require at least two years of evidence.

Progression rates through the threshold can vary between schools.

KNOW YOUR WORTH TO MAXIMISE YOUR SALARY (TOP SECRET)

The perception in relation to teachers' pay is that after qualifying, all teachers start on Main Scale Pay Point 1 (M1) and each year progress up one level if they meet their performance management targets, until they reach M6.

This is a myth.

A contract is a negotiation between yourself and the school. Depending on the strength of your hand, whether you teach maths, P.E., computer science or geography, your negotiating power can be considerable. In subjects where there is a significant shortage, the demand for your services will be huge. Schools are under pressure to get specialists teaching their subject. In shortage subjects, you need to know your worth.

At the time of writing, the annual cost difference between an outgoing experienced teacher at the top of the Upper Pay Scale (UPS3, £40,490) and a teacher starting at the bottom of the ladder on the Main Scale (M1, £24,373) is roughly £16,000 (salary scales up to August 2020). I'm referring to the basic salary, not including the extra costs that the school has to pay on top, such as national insurance, employer's pension contributions and any allowances for additional responsibilities.

Now, you may be thinking that this is understandable, because the teacher on the higher salary is being paid more for their experience. You could be right. But you could be wrong.

When you arrive at your new school, you may soon

discover that the teacher next door who has been teaching for 20 years (UPS3) is not much better than yourself. In fact, you might be doing a better job than them. Now, if I told you they were earning £16,000 a year more than you, you are not likely to be that happy. This situation arises because under the old system with its automatic movement through the main scale each year, higher pay could be the result of long service rather than excellence. Headteachers aren't telling you this, for obvious reasons.

If you are applying for a position, the teacher that you replace may have been a high earner. When a trainee teacher accepts a job on M1, it is an excellent saving for the school. If you realise this, you are more likely to be confident at knowing your worth.

How do I capitalise on this?

Clearly, headteachers need to save costs, as the amount of money they receive has not increased in line with cost pressures for many years. Yet there are benefits to be had if you know your worth and are courageous.

For many trainee teachers, a teaching job may be their first 'proper job' and an interview panel can be daunting. Negotiating your pay may also feel awkward. The only way to get over it is by asking; the first time is always the hardest.

What you should remember is that the colleagues on the interview panel will have done exactly the same thing. The headteacher negotiates their own salary with the governors, and the Head of Department will have negotiated their salary. If they haven't, that's their problem.

There are different ways to do this, some more effective than others. Be realistic; if you're a trainee teacher and you ask to be put onto the Upper Pay Scale straight away, you will probably be laughed at. It shows you don't understand that your impact needs to be 'significant and sustained' before you apply for this. However, I would argue that any range within M1-6 could be achievable. If you're a maths teacher, some schools may be tempted to offer you a large salary, especially if you are an exceptional candidate. This all comes back to knowing your worth.

If, on interview day, you believe you are one of the strongest candidates there, your negotiation stance may improve. If there is stiff competition, your position may be weaker.

WHEN DO I DO THIS?

The time to negotiate your salary usually comes at the end of the interview, when they ask if you have any questions. As mentioned, negotiating your salary for the first time can be uncomfortable, but you must acknowledge that the people on the panel opposite will almost certainly have attempted it during their careers. It is part of any contract negotiation at any business on the planet. For some reason, many teachers seem to just take what they're given.

HOW DO I ASK?

A risky strategy is to say that you have other interviews lined up and will only be able to accept the job for a certain amount, M3 for example. The headteacher may be constrained by the pay policy or could regard your request as too bold. I would argue that if you have done your research, you will know your value.

Some headteachers don't like you asking because it goes against their school pay policy. But remember, certain positions are more difficult to fill than others, which may strengthen your hand. If you are a maths teacher asking for your first salary to be M3 instead of M1, and you are turned down... trust me, the school down the road will snap your arm off if you are half decent.

A softer approach might be to explain that you know your value. Say that you have another couple of interviews to attend and were wondering if there was any negotiation available considering the school's pay policy. A headteacher may then come back to you and ask what salary you're looking for. When you respond, they may say it isn't possible for whatever reason or offer you a salary they think is appropriate. You have then opened the conversation and can discuss it from there. Remember, know your worth.

If your type of post or subject is in demand and you are a strong trainee teacher applying for a shortage subject, but you are paid on M1 for your first job, you have probably missed a trick. It will impact on your next job as well: instead of applying for another job from a position of a higher salary, you will be on a lower one, which will make future negotiations harder. Bite the bullet, ask politely and you may be surprised at what can be offered.

Just remember not to be too big-headed about it, thinking your value is higher than it actually is. If you're a teacher in a field of strong candidates and you go in saying you couldn't accept the job unless they offer UPS3, you might as well not have turned up.

I would end the conversation by stating a minimum salary that you need in order to accept. This makes sure the headteacher knows where they stand.

Top Tip: Know your worth. At the end of the interview, ask the panel if there is room for negotiation of the starting salary within the remit of the school's pay policy. This shows that you know your worth, while understanding that they may be constrained by their school's policy, and it opens up the negotiation process quite nicely. You can then freely discuss where both parties stand. Finish the negotiation by stating a minimum salary at which you'd accept the job. #TeachingTopTip

ON THE PHONE LATER

If you said that you could start the job on a given salary, say M3, and the headteacher rings you back and says they'd like to offer you M2, remember to stand your ground. I can't give individual advice here, because every job will be different and every negotiation will end differently; but if you said your minimum was M3, try your best to stick to it. If the worst happens and the headteacher says if you can't do M2 they will have to withdraw the offer, you will still start on M2 instead of M1. It's a nice increase anyway, more than if you hadn't asked!

A WORD OF CAUTION

If you don't negotiate your pay during the interview, you won't always be able to start negotiating on the phone after-wards. If you were that concerned about the pay, you should have raised it earlier; the headteacher may need approval from their board, governors or other regulatory bodies before they can discuss it over the phone.

If you want to negotiate pay, make sure it doesn't come as a surprise to the headteacher at the very last stage. Discuss it in the interview panel and see how the conversation goes.

DOUBLE JUMPS WITHIN PERFORMANCE RELATED PAY (PRP)

Once you accept a job and are working within the performance related pay structure at your current school, you are likely to be given three targets to meet in order to move up the pay scale the following year. At the start of the process, you may be able to request a 'double jump'; this means that if you meet additional targets or perform exceptionally well, you could qualify for accelerated pay progression.

Again, headteachers don't commonly broadcast this because they may want to keep costs down, but it is useful for teachers to know. It will all be explained in the school's pay policy and you should definitely read it to check what is and isn't possible.

FINAL NOTE ON PAY

I must stress that not everyone knows the information you've read in this chapter. Your mentors, Heads of Department and colleagues may not be aware of it. Headteachers rarely publicise this information, to prevent an influx of staff asking for double jumps or to move onto the UPS without being on M6 first, even though it will be explicitly stated in your school's pay policy. It doesn't mean they wouldn't ask if they were in your position again.

It is useful intelligence and I hope it helps some of you receive a much bigger starting salary than you had thought was possible!

PERSONAL PRODUCTIVITY

Managing your workload is crucial. Too many teachers are slaves to the profession; you must avoid this and maintain a work-life balance. I suppose the nature of the job, helping pupils to be the best person they can be, attracts a certain type of individual. Teachers are special and they care deeply about their work.

But we must not forget our limits; we have our own lives to lead. Partners, children, friends and family are often our priority and we must be careful not to push ourselves so far that our work-life balance is destroyed.

I have had first-hand experience of teachers in their training years who arrive into school before the gates open at 7am. They are kicked out by the caretakers at 6pm, go home, and then continue working until late in the evening. This routine is unsustainable and ridiculous. Much better time management is required.

The first piece of advice I will give to you is to keep in mind Parkinson's law: work expands to fill the time available for completion. What does this mean? If you have ten minutes to complete a task, you will complete it in ten minutes. If you have an hour to complete the same task, it will take you one hour. This principle is vital for teachers to know and understand. Never mistake being busy for being productive. You could spend an entire day in the library doing 'work' but realise afterwards that you have not achieved much. It is far better to be productive than busy.

Lesson planning can take forever at the beginning of your teaching career and learning how to plan is essential. But use your mentors, teachers in your department, to help find resources and plan your lessons. There is no point in trying to figure it all out yourself when teachers in the department can do it ten times faster or pass on existing materials. You can then use your time to plan how to teach the subject rather than searching for the resources you need. Lesson planning is so much more important than lesson resourcing.

Time management is so personal that it is difficult to give specific advice on it. It has to work for you. But I would stress that you must make and keep boundaries. It is far better that pupils have a teacher who is well rested, energetic and fresh with an average lesson than sit through a superb lesson delivered by someone who is short tempered, tired and sleep deprived. You should aim for a balance all the time.

Looking at this from the perspective of Parkinson's law, you will take longer to plan lessons in your training year because you simply have more time to plan them. With a reduced timetable, planning one lesson may take you an hour because you have one hour available to plan the lesson. Having the time to spend doing an activity can actually decrease your productivity. When you become qualified, you can't spend as long planning because you simply have less time to plan as the number of lessons you are required to teach increases. If you move into leadership, time will be in even shorter supply, because of your additional responsibilities. Try and set yourself short, mini deadlines to ensure you don't spend too long completing activities and you keep your productivity high.

TIPS TO MANAGE YOUR WORKLOAD

MAKE A TO DO LIST FOR THE FOLLOWING DAY

Before you go to bed, make a list of the key priorities that you must do tomorrow. This will help you become focused for the day ahead and will ensure you prioritise tasks rather than waiting until the day itself when you have a lot to do. If you need to solve any problems, setting them out on paper the night before allows your subconscious to work on them while you're asleep. You will be amazed that by writing your thoughts and tasks down beforehand, you are more prepared to tackle the tasks when you wake up.

If you go through a day without having identified your priorities, you will find yourself completing lots of meaningless work without a clear direction for what you are trying to achieve. Instead, by noting key targets and items that need to be completed the following day, you will have a sense of purpose when you set out and you can anticipate a sense of achievement when they are accomplished. You will therefore make sure that these take precedence over the more menial, less impactful tasks you might otherwise have done.

E-MAILS

Turn off school e-mail notifications. I strongly recommend checking your e-mails three times a day to start with. I check mine first thing in the morning to see if there is anything I need to attend to, but I only ever act on these e-mails if they are urgent; all other requests can wait. At lunch time, I do a scan for any urgent messages to address, ignoring the remainder. Finally, I look again at the end of the day.

During the working day, any spare time is used to tick off items from the To Do list I made the night before. This approach is far more productive than spending my time answering e-mails. The majority of e-mails will represent wasted time and wasted productivity.

By the end of the school day, I have built up a batch of e-mails that I can get rid of or action promptly. By batching them up, I have saved many minutes of looking at my e-mails at various points and answering them one by one. Instead, what I can now do is rifle through them, skim reading and ignoring any that don't require action on my part.

It is too tempting to reply to e-mails as soon as they arrive in your inbox. The minutes you spend refreshing your inbox, drafting and re-drafting responses soon accumulates; and it is surprising how much time you can waste checking your mail.

It is interesting to see how managers reply to emails compared to other teachers. Managers often reply with no introduction, but simply a one-sentence response to a question. Or simply, a 'Yes', 'No', or 'Ok.' It is because managers value their time. They do not respond with a long-winded, 'Dear Ed, I gratefully received your e-mail earlier. I am afraid... Yours sincerely,' because it takes too long. E-mail is not meant to be a protracted form of communication. It should be short and snappy.

As a teacher, try and batch your e-mails together and get straight to the point. Discretion is advised; there may be particular people where a direct approach makes you feel uncomfortable, so there is still room for flexibility.

For those who are scared of missing something vital, I've

always found that if a message is serious enough, someone will come and find me.

Learn to say 'no'

As a keen, enthusiastic and determined teacher (which I know you are because you're reading this book), you will be asked to do lots of things within the school environment. Remember to look after yourself and say 'No' more times than 'Yes'.

One tip is to get a diary and write 'No' in every single page. That way, when you're asked if you can do something, you have an extra incentive to turn it down if required.

There may be opportunities that you would like to get involved in, and that's great, but only take up those that you are really interested in. This sounds selfish, but you have to act this way, otherwise you will end up with too much on your plate to the detriment of your core role.

There will be some teachers drowning in things to do, looking for young, enthusiastic teachers to take aspects of their workload. Don't be naïve and think this doesn't happen. Be cautious when accepting work or requests from colleagues and think carefully before you say 'Yes' to everything.

By all means, get stuck into things at school and offer to help where you want to, but don't just say 'Yes' because you want to please people. Do it because you want to. Otherwise, you will face a mountain of extra work that you begrudge.

Top Tip: 'No' in your diary. Write 'No' on every page of your diary. When asked to do something, it always gives you that little extra motivation to turn down the opportunity. Learning how to say no will improve your productivity, letting you focus on the opportunities you are keen to take up. **#TeachingTopTip**

PERSONAL WELLBEING

LOOKING AFTER YOURSELF

YOUR TIME IS PRECIOUS

I remember speaking to one of my ex-colleagues about procrastinating at work. He never seemed to engage in small talk with colleagues. I remember asking him why, and his answers resonated with me.

He said, 'Every minute I spend with people at work talking about things is a minute less to speak to my wife when I arrive back at home, or a minute less to spend with my daughter before we put her to bed at night.' Now, some may say that this can go too far and that it can lead to teachers hiding away in their rooms as hermits, but I don't think anyone could argue they were unaware of this teacher's priorities. He had a tremendous work-life balance, was an excellent leader and a superb practitioner. I have always remembered it, and I think it is something for us all to reflect on. What are our priorities?

Teachers like to talk, and you have to remind yourself that your time is precious. By all means chat to colleagues and catch up with them about their weekends, but use your time wisely and make sure you don't become unproductive, leaving all of your lesson planning until late at night. It is a common mistake I see too often.

Remember earlier, when I said 'Never spend more time on an activity than it will take the pupils to complete.' Cutting out, laminating an activity and spending an hour animating slides which only take five minutes to watch seems like an inefficient use of time. Don't be drawn into thinking you have to do huge amounts of work; it is unsustainable and could lead to burnout.

Clearly, there is a danger that you could become so productive that you ignore everyone else and become absorbed in your own little world with no social contact. It is not about one extreme as opposed to the other, but it is about making sure that you carry out your priorities.

TAKE CARE OF YOUR WORKING HOURS

Teaching is a job where you could work 24 hours a day and still have things to do. There is an endless To Do list and you face continuous expectations from colleagues, school leaders and pupils, so you must prioritise. The most important thing is to look after yourself. Everything else takes a back seat I'm afraid. Yes, there will be other things that you are asked to do, but your health comes first. Without you, there is no lesson; always remember that. The second most important thing is to deliver good lessons for the pupils. The bread and butter of teaching is delivering good lessons, day in, day out.

It might seem fun designing colour coded spreadsheets and doing a host of other tasks, but these are a form of procrastination. Sort yourself and your lessons first, then worry about everything else. Too many teachers who struggle in the classroom find prioritisation difficult. I have seen teachers struggling with their classes, finding it difficult to plan lessons where pupils learn their intended outcomes, but then I discover they have been working until late at night in the staff room making sure that the topic test scores are perfectly displayed in a spreadsheet, with colour co-ordinated conditional formatting, titles, animations and a whole suite of statistical analysis. They have missed the point; all of this comes after delivering good lessons in the classroom. Procrastination is the enemy.

Look after yourself. Most 'newbie' teachers seem to broadcast their hours as a badge of honour. It's not. Staying up until midnight planning your lessons for the following day is not something to be proud of; it isn't helpful either for you or the pupils. You will be exhausted, will go to your lessons tired and will take out your frustration on pupils.

This is why it's so important you get your bog-standard lesson sorted. Fast.

CREATING YOUR 'BOG-STANDARD' LESSON

Everyone dreams of having the best lessons, where the pupils talk about you as their favourite teacher and how you are just fabulous. What you will soon realise out when you start teaching is that you only have a limited amount of time in a day.

Creating amazing, awe-inspiring lessons takes time and not everyone can afford to do it. We spoke earlier in the book about the focus needing to be on the pupils' learning and not whether pupils are busy in the lesson. A 'fun' lesson is not necessarily one in which pupils learn anything. It is important to remember that.

Instead, you need to find your 'basic' lesson, fast. Teachers cannot be entertainers throughout the whole day, five or six lessons a day; it is not feasible. Instead, I find the best teachers are the ones who are consistent, teaching solid lessons day in, day out. They don't blow the doors off with excitement, but they are rock steady, every day. As a new teacher into the classroom, you should know that this is fine and is in fact expected. Yes, with your enthusiasm you will want to make every lesson fantastic, but it is not going to happen. Get over it.

Your job is to teach pupils, and pupils need to learn which is the most important thing. Of course, if you want to experiment and make some of your lessons more interesting than others, that is to be encouraged, but don't imagine that expert teaching is doing that for every lesson, every day.

After you have been teaching for a few weeks or a month, reflect on what your basic standard lesson looks like and be sure to do many of these. This will allow you the time to plan, mark and have a life outside of teaching, which is so important for long-term sustainability in teaching your classes.

When planning your lessons, think about what your pupils need to learn, how they are going to learn it and how are you going to assess it. These three components will help you understand what you're aiming for. Trust me, it needn't be anything fancy.

STAY POSITIVE

We have discussed the need to stay positive in teaching. It is a wonderful profession and you will experience many highs as part of your career. Inevitably, there will be moments where you think a lesson didn't go that well, or a pupil will say something to you that is hurtful. Build your resilience by recognising that these moments will come, but that they are only temporary and there will be better times ahead.

A useful strategy to help in these situations is to keep a positivity drawer. As a teacher, you will receive cards, presents, nice e-mails, notes and thank you cards from teachers and pupils over time. Keep hold of them. Store them in a drawer. Teaching can be emotional and hard at times, and having a drawer full of positives is always nice to dip into from time to time. It can evoke happy memories of events in the past and messages from pupils can remind you why you are in the profession.

Top Tip: Keep a positivity drawer. Keep hold of the positivity you receive and store it away for a time when you're feeling low. It helps remind you of past memories and helps you understand any blip in morale is only temporary. Better times will return. Teaching is a wonderful profession. **#TeachingTopTip**

Unfortunately, no matter how hard we may try to keep ourselves positive, there are some teachers out there who unfortunately just like to moan. Pupils and other staff wonder why they are still teaching. They have lost the passion they once (hopefully) had and are now spreading their negativity around the school.

I find that negativity is common within school staff rooms. In one school I worked at, I made a conscious effort to avoid the staff room at certain times of the day. It sounds over the top, but I wanted to surround myself with positivity. I am not interested in the 'glory days' of 40 years ago or moaning about my boss or the headteacher. Whenever you find yourself talking to a 'moaner', I urge you to find the politest way to finish the conversation and avoid speaking to them in the future. They can affect your mood and are best avoided.

Top Tip: Avoid negativity. There are some teachers who are more negative than others. They like to moan, and they can bring your morale down if you are not careful. Try to surround yourself with positive people and if you do find yourself speaking to someone who likes to moan, close the conversation down and move on to speak to someone else. #TeachingTopTip

---

MR WATSON, NOT 'ED'

At first, it was weird to be called by my teacher name, 'Mr Watson'. I had never been called that in my life, but all of a sudden, pupils knew me by that name. After a while, I realised how important this distinction was. I am not there to be their friend, I am a role model and I am there to teach them. I not only teach them my subject but also aim to support their personal development to become rounded individuals.

At times, even though you invest so much time into your pupils, some pupils will let you down and insult you or say something harmful. This is where making a distinction between your identities will help you deal with a situation. They are releasing their frustration at Mr Watson, that person who teaches them maths, or who told them off for chewing gum in the lesson. They are *not* having a go at 'Ed.' Ed is someone completely different to Mr Watson. Ed has his own life, his own friends and his own social circles; pupils are not having a go at him.

Top Tip: Create your teacher persona. When pupils are being hurtful, they are attacking your teacher persona, not you personally. Brush it off. It's not about you as a person, but about the teacher who may or may not have told them off. #TeachingTopTip

---

WHAT IF THEY DELIBERATELY CALL ME BY MY FIRST NAME?

If pupils call you by your first name, join the club. This has probably happened to every teacher who has ever taught. How to react will depend on the teacher and the context in which it was said.

I find the best way to respond is with a bit of humour, showing that it doesn't bother me in any way. If you give pupils the tiniest hint that you don't like it, before you know it, large numbers of pupils will be calling you by your first name from across the corridor, in the canteen and outside, and you'll find it impossible to punish or identify everyone.

From experience, you should strive to give the impression that it does not faze you at all and over time the pupils will just get bored and move on to something else. By reacting, you give them the entertainment they may have been looking for, and it will just make the situation worse.

· · ·

CONTINUE YOUR HOBBIES

Many people will tell you that teacher training and your first year in teaching are so intense you won't have any time for anything else. This view usually comes from a teacher who didn't manage their time effectively and could not prioritise.

You must continue your hobbies. Whether it's continuing to play hockey on the weekend, playing in an orchestra, swimming, or whatever you prefer, you must continue it, as it presumably gives you joy. Looking after yourself is crucial; devoting your entire life to teaching can be harmful and lead to burnout.

Yes, you will be busy when you start at a school for the first time, but it doesn't mean you have to stop having a life. Continue your hobbies. It will keep you grounded, will give you something to look forward to and will force you to get your work done beforehand.

CONCLUSION

Now is an appropriate time to recap everything we've learned so far. We started by exploring the qualities of excellent teachers and how to develop your ideal classroom culture. Following this, we looked into the power of observing others and being observed yourself to improve and shape your own classroom environment, before discussing how to use your own personality to develop effective relationships with pupils.

An insight into behaviour management and tips to improve your classroom control followed, including the effective use of routines and the need to apply rules consistently. Understandably, managing behaviour is one of the main worries and anxieties for teachers new to the profession, but hopefully this book has helped you by suggesting some strategies to help you excel within the classroom.

We then looked at pedagogy and the need to plan lessons as a sequence rather than as singular units. Not only does this help to ensure each lesson links to the previous one and the one that will come next, but it also saves time on lesson planning. We realised the folly of spending hours and hours animating PowerPoint slides when it will have no impact; you should not spend more time preparing an activity than it will take for the pupils to complete it. Linked to this, we identified that many 'recommended activities' such as Treasure hunts, tarsias and more interactive approaches often give the illusion of pupils learning when they are only having fun. Never mistake activity for achievement.

After this, we explored general teaching processes and how to take responsibility for your career development, noting that you should try and view all criticism as constructive. People who critique your work and offer suggestions for improvement are those who care. Always try to remember that they want to see you improve.

We identified the need to invest in yourself continually. Look for opportunities to grow, learn and take on more responsibility. Remember, no one cares about your career as much as you do, so take ownership of it. Be proactive and search out opportunities; you will become an essential part of the staff workforce and more opportunities will come your way.

We moved on to look at finding your first job, taking you through an interview process and what an interview day looks like. Remember that you are on show from the minute you arrive at the school to the minute you leave. Know how to conduct yourself in the best possible way, ensure that your interview lesson is as planned as possible and be constantly reflective. We discussed how to negotiate starting salaries and the need to know your worth but be humble in how you approach the negotiation. We examined how to move from one job to the next, ensuring you comply with policies and procedures without causing unnecessary grief or problems for your superiors.

Finally, we touched on maximising your productivity and

personal wellbeing. Teaching is a wonderful profession, but it can be very busy at times. Like any job, there are pinch points, but if you keep to a routine and look after yourself first, everything else will follow. The minute you stop taking care of yourself, you start a downward spiral that it is difficult to get out of. Look after number one.

You may not have been able to take in all of the information within this book before you start to teach, so please use it as a reference tool to dip in and out of in your early career. It will provide the support and strategies to enable you to excel at teaching in the shortest possible time.

FINAL REMARKS

This book has been the culmination of years spent developing my own practice and that of others. It is the best guide I can offer you to start your wonderful profession in teaching. I hope that it is useful for you as you take the first steps in your teaching career.

If you enjoyed this book and believe some of the advice might be useful for other colleagues in the profession, I'd love to hear about it! Please leave a review wherever you bought the book and share it with colleagues. Why not think of five colleagues or friends who would benefit from reading it and write their names down, right now? Then make a pledge to yourself to let them know about this book and they will be able to gain some of the advice you have taken from this book themselves.

The teaching profession can be life-changing. We have the opportunity to transform pupils' lives and ensure that any pupil from any background can stand as an equal in any circle and take up any opportunity. Through excellent teaching and learning, we can make sure that every child can achieve academic and behavioural excellence and achieve more than they ever thought possible.

Finally, remember to smile. Teaching is a rollercoaster. Not only will you feel like you're riding an emotional roller-coaster within a term, but you will also experience it within a week, a day and even a lesson. Teaching is a phenomenal profession and the impact that you have on children's lives will make all of the hard work worth it.

I wish you well and look forward to hearing from you in the future!

Take care

@MrEdWatson

ACKNOWLEDGEMENTS

I'd like to thank all the teachers who I have been fortunate enough to take notes from, observe and ask for advice. They have shaped my knowledge and helped me to improve my teaching practice and share ideas with others.

Overall, there are too many people to thank who have supported me in my teaching journey to date. But above all, I must acknowledge David Stewart, Stuart Trutch, Charlie Berney, Lucy Wenham, Matt Stevenson, my family and most importantly Hannah for their tremendous support.

I would also like to thank my editor, Julie Cordiner, for her suggestions and advice, and for improving the quality of my work.

ABOUT THE AUTHOR

Originally from Gloucester, Ed has taught in some of England's most challenging schools, most recently in Bristol. He trained as a maths teacher, before becoming Head of Department and is moving into a senior leadership post overseeing whole school teaching and learning later this year.

His drive and determination stems from his wish that no pupil should be limited in what they can achieve, no matter which establishment they attend or where they were born. Instead, with the right support, training and teachers, every pupil can achieve academic, behavioural and cultural excellence that will enable them to stand as equals in any circle and make the most of any opportunity.

Contact Ed:
    Twitter: https://twitter.com/MrEdWatson
    LinkedIn: www.linkedin.com/in/mredwatson
    Website: www.mredwatson.com

Printed in Great Britain
by Amazon